THE PROPHET
AND HIS WORK

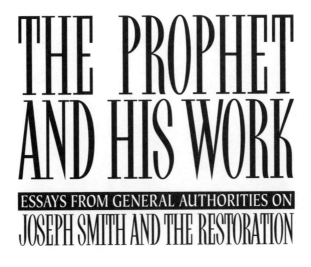

THE PROPHET AND HIS WORK

ESSAYS FROM GENERAL AUTHORITIES ON

JOSEPH SMITH AND THE RESTORATION

DESERET BOOK COMPANY, SALT LAKE CITY, UTAH

Library of Congress Cataloging-in-Publication Data

The prophet and his work : essays from general authorities on Joseph Smith and the restoration.
    p.   cm.
  Includes bibliographical references and index.
  ISBN 1-57345-193-2 (hardbound)
  1. Smith, Joseph, 1805–1844. 2. Church of Jesus Christ of Latter-day Saints—Doctrines. 3. Mormon Church—Doctrines.
BX8695.S6P75   1996
289.3'092—dc20   96-22251
                                              CIP

Printed in the United States of America

10 9   8   7   6   5   4   3   2   1

CONTENTS

CONTENTS

INTRODUCTION

Some 2,000 years before the birth of Christ, Joseph of Egypt prophesied of Joseph Smith, Jr.—an unschooled plowboy in nineteenth-century America who would become the prophet through which God would restore the gospel of Jesus Christ to the earth. "His name shall be called after me; and it shall be after the name of his father. And . . . the thing, which the Lord shall bring forth by his hand, . . . shall bring my people unto salvation" (2 Nephi 3:15).

In 1844, almost 2,000 years *after* the birth of Christ, John Taylor declared that "Joseph Smith . . . has done more, save Jesus only, for the salvation of men in this world, than any other man that ever lived in it" (D&C 135:3).

For literally thousands of years, prophets of God have testified with boldness about the life, mission, and divinely inspired work of Joseph Smith. It is in this tradition that we present this collection of essays.

The collection covers a wide range of topics concerning the Prophet, from personal testimonies of him, to details about his life and ministry, to his role in the larger gospel picture of the Apostasy and Restoration.

Written by General Authorities of the Church, the essays center on personal conviction of Joseph Smith's calling as a prophet of God and the profound importance of his life and work.

We see Joseph from the time he was a small boy to the hour of his martyrdom. President James E. Faust and Elder Joseph B. Wirthlin show us in-depth the Prophet's associations with his family and friends, including his relationship with his brother Hyrum and his love for his parents, wife, and children. Of Hyrum, Joseph said, "I love him with that love that is stronger than death, for I never had occasion to rebuke him, nor he me."

Joseph Smith's leadership, service, and love for his fellowmen are legendary. In Thomas S. Monson's essay, "Teacher by Example," we read about the Prophet calling John Page to serve a mission in Canada. Brother Page responded, "'Why, Brother Joseph, I can't go on a mission to Canada. I don't even have a coat to wear.' The Prophet Joseph took his own coat from his back, handed it to John Page, and said, 'Here, John, wear this, and the Lord will bless you.'" In Neal A. Maxwell's essay, "Joseph, The Seer," we learn how Joseph risked his life for a young man by carrying him upon his shoulders through swamp and darkness as a mob pursued them. A letter to Jared Carter from the Prophet reads, "I love your soul, and the souls of the children of men, and pray and do all that I can for the salvation of all."

In addition to showing Joseph as a remarkable man, the authors forthrightly proclaim him as a prophet, seer, and revelator of God. Joseph's contributions as a prophet are also acclaimed by prominent scholars who are not members of the Church. For example, Elder Joe J. Christensen quotes Dr. Harold Bloom, a distinguished professor at Yale University: "I also do not find it possible to doubt that Joseph Smith was an authentic prophet. Where in all of American history can we find his match?"

Many essays included in this collection focus on the Apostasy and Restoration. Elder Dallin H. Oaks and Elder F. Enzio Busche write clearly about gospel truths that were lost or changed after the time of Christ, differences between our church and other Christian churches, and why the Restoration was necessary. Other essays discuss in detail the beautiful truths of the gospel that were restored. For example, in the essay entitled "Oh, How Lovely Was the Morning!" Elder Carlos E. Asay highlights ten eternal truths we learn from the First Vision. In "Our Message to the World," Elder Robert E. Wells places Joseph Smith as part of the Christ-focused message of Latter-day Saints to the world and states, "When one studies the doctrinal teachings revealed to Joseph Smith, that person, if he or she is sincere in the search for truth, will be led to Jesus Christ."

Varied in scope, *The Prophet and His Work* includes unusual works not often found in a collection about Joseph Smith. For example, Elder M. Russell Ballard, a descendant of Hyrum Smith, writes about the life of the Prophet's brother. And in the chapter "At the Heart of the Church," Elder Russell M. Nelson helps us prepare for attacks that may be made against the Prophet.

Ultimately, though, the thrust of these essays is the personal testimony each of our leaders offers of Joseph Smith. "I have never forgotten that moment in my life," says President Gordon B. Hinckley of one of the formative experiences in his testimony of Joseph. "I was an awkward, freckled-faced little boy in knee pants, more prone to laugh than to be serious. But on this occasion, I felt a great moving power. It was both emotional and spiritual, . . . its testimony has become my own testimony." Many of the authors have traveled to the sites of Joseph Smith's history, where the Father and the Son appeared to Joseph, where the plates were hidden up, where the first temple of this dispensation was built. They have been to Liberty, where Joseph suffered and was comforted by the Lord, and to Carthage, where Joseph and Hyrum were brutally killed. They have fasted, they have prayed, and they have searched their own souls and found the deeply personal conviction that Joseph Smith is a prophet of God. It is to this truth that each of them testify.

Adding to the testimonies of prophets and apostles for centuries, *The Prophet and His Work* offers vibrant new insights into the life and work of Joseph Smith.

AS ONE WHO LOVES THE PROPHET

PRESIDENT GORDON B. HINCKLEY

I have chosen to write not as a scholar, but simply as one who loves a most uncommon man who was known by the common name of Joseph Smith.

May I tell you of some of the reasons for that love? I grew up in a home where there was love for the Prophet. That home included a substantial library. When we were ever so small our mother read to us from two books. They were titled *From Plough Boy to Prophet* and *Mother Stories from the Book of Mormon*. They were written by William A. Morton, who knew how to put words together so that children could understand and enjoy them. We also read from a small volume, published in 1900, titled *The Latter-day Prophet, History of Joseph Smith*. It was written for young people by George Q. Cannon. It is, in fact, a synopsis of the monumental life of the Prophet. Our library also contained a little red-cover book, *Joseph Smith's Teachings*, compiled and published by Edwin F. Parry in 1912. It likewise contained

Joseph Smith the Prophet, written by his mother, Lucy Mack Smith. On two small tables stood two statues, each about twenty-six to thirty inches high. One was a miniature of the Joseph Smith statue by Mahonri Young, which stands on Temple Square. The other was a statue of Abraham Lincoln. I grew up in an environment of appreciation for the Prophet.

When I was twelve years of age, I was ordained a deacon. That would have been in 1922. My father had served as a counselor in the stake presidency and was named stake president about that time. A stake priesthood meeting was held each month. It was held on a week night in the old Tenth Ward building, which still stands on the corner of Fourth South and Eighth East in Salt Lake City. Father said that since I now held the priesthood, I should attend stake priesthood meeting with him. It was with some reluctance that I put on my best clothes and walked with him to the Tenth Ward. He sat on the stand and I sat on the back row. The hall was filled with men, with only a few boys. Quite a number of immigrants from Europe lived in the stake, men who had paid a heavy price for their membership in the Church and who carried in their hearts a strong conviction of its truth. The opening hymn was announced. All stood and sang:

> Praise to the man who communed with Jehovah!
> Jesus anointed that Prophet and Seer.
> Blessed to open the last dispensation,
> Kings shall extol him, and nations revere.
> (*Hymns,* 1985, no. 27)

The chapel rang with the words of that great hymn. It was sung with conviction and intensity by men who carried in their hearts a powerful testimony of the prophetic calling of him of whom they sang.

I have never forgotten that moment in my life. I was an awkward, freckled-faced little boy in knee pants, more prone to laugh than to be serious. But on this occasion, I felt a great moving power. It was both emotional and spiritual. Ever since, that hymn has held a special place in my heart, and its testimony has become my own testimony.

> Great is his glory and endless his priesthood.
> Ever and ever the keys he will hold.
> Faithful and true, he will enter his kingdom,
> Crowned in the midst of the prophets of old.

When I was about fourteen or fifteen, my brother and I would accompany our parents to the general conferences held in the Tabernacle. At that time there was room for everyone who wished to get in.

Heber J. Grant was President of the Church. In imagination, I can still see and hear him. He stood tall. He did not read from a manuscript. He spoke from his heart. His voice rang out in moving words of testimony concerning Joseph Smith and the Book of Mormon.

From these and other experiences of my younger years, there came accretions of knowledge and faith concerning the Prophet Joseph. Was there ever doubt? Yes, admittedly at times, particularly in my university days. That was a time of general cynicism. It was the bottom of the Great Depression, a depression so deep and severe that later recessions, by comparison, seem to be seasons of prosperity.

I read in those days, and have since read, much of the writing leveled against the Prophet by critics, not a few, who have worn out their lives trying, honestly or dishonestly, to find some flaw of character, some note of history to destroy the credibility of Joseph Smith. I am grateful to say that I have survived them all, and that the more I have read, the stronger have grown my faith in and my love for this most remarkable and wonderful man. His detractors, without exception insofar as I know, have had their day in the sun, and then have faded into oblivion, while the name of Joseph Smith has been honored in ever-widening circles around the earth.

I thank him, I honor him, I love him for the faith, simple and trusting, that impelled him to go into the grove to ask of God, "nothing doubting." From that experience came knowledge of Deity beyond any comprehended by the learned of the world through centuries of time.

God, he learned, is indeed in form like a man. He hears. He speaks. He introduces His Beloved Son and directs Joseph to listen. The Son speaks, even the Resurrected Lord Jesus Christ, the Firstborn of the Father, and the Savior and Redeemer of the world. He, too, is in form like a man. He counsels the boy before Them.

Those to whom Joseph told this wondrous story ridiculed him. I thank him and love him for the courage to stand up to those who were much his senior and who mercilessly condemned him.

"For I had seen a vision;" he said, "I knew it, and I knew that God knew it, and I could not deny it, neither dared I do it; at least I knew that by so doing I would offend God, and come under condemnation" (JS–H 1:25).

Because of his experience and his testimony I know to whom I may go in prayer, petitioning the Father in the name of His Beloved Son.

I thank Joseph the Prophet and love him for the Book of Mormon, this added testament of Jesus Christ, a record that has come forth from the dust to bring understanding and knowledge, strength and faith, to all who will read it prayerfully, and into whose hearts will come confirmation of the living reality of the Son of God, the Savior and Redeemer of the world. This book and its translator were attacked even before it issued from the press, and it has been attacked ever since. Scores of explanations have been given for it in an effort to refute the Prophet's story. But the test of its truth lies in its reading, and it is being read more widely than at any time in its history. More than three million copies are printed in a single year. What a contrast with that first edition of five thousand copies, the printing of which was made possible by a generous farmer upon whom the Spirit of the Lord rested.

The Book of Mormon recently was rated the eighth most influential book in America. It was tied with number six and number seven. The Bible was number one, and I have not the slightest doubt that at some future time this companion scripture will become number two, second only to the Bible, and every individual who reads it will be the better for the effort, for, as Joseph said, " . . . a man would get nearer to God by abiding by its precepts, than by any other book" (Book of Mormon, Introduction).

I thank him and love him for the holy priesthood restored upon his head by those who held it anciently. I thank him for the Aaronic Priesthood, which holds "the keys of the ministering of angels, and of the gospel of repentance, and of baptism by immersion for the remission of sins" (D&C 13). I thank him for the Melchizedek Priesthood, with all of its powers, keys, and authority. It is the divine power of the Almighty conferred upon man to act in His name and in His stead. It is efficacious in life, and its authority reaches beyond the veil of death. It is the only power on the earth that may be exercised by man to seal and bind for eternity as well as for time. How remarkable and precious a boon it is.

I thank the Prophet Joseph and love him for the doctrine of salvation, which was revealed through him. Through the grace of God all men will be privileged to rise from the dead, a gift freely given and made possible through the atoning sacrifice of the Lord Jesus Christ. Beyond this, all who walk in obedience to the teachings and commandments of the gospel may go on, even to exaltation. There are various kingdoms and principalities in the life beyond, named and described in the incomparable divine revelations that came through him. I thank him and love him for all of this. I love him for the assurance, certain and unequivocal, of life after death in a realm of activity and growth, in contrast with a condition of static and unfruitful ecstasy as others have taught. How grateful I am for the grandeur of his vision of eternity. I thank him for the assurance that, "mingling with Gods, he can plan for his brethren."

I thank him and love him for the sealing power of the holy priesthood that makes possible and certain the continuance of the family through eternity. I have said many times that if nothing else came out of all of the sorrow and travail and pain of the Restoration than the sealing power of the holy priesthood to bind together families forever, it would have been worth all that it has cost.

I thank him and love him for the light and understanding he brought to the world concerning the purpose of life—that mortality is a step in an eternal journey, that we lived before we came here, that there was design in our coming, that we are sons and daughters of God our Eternal Father with a divine and wonderful birthright, that we are here to be tested and to grow, that, as one man has said, "Life is a mission and not a career," that death is a step across the threshold into another realm as real and as purposeful as this. Infinite is our opportunity to grow toward godhood under the plan of our Eternal Father and His Beloved Son.

I thank him and love him for temporal teachings and programs of infinite worth. I am thankful for what we call the Word of Wisdom. It is true that others of his time were interested in diet as it affects health. But none of whom I am aware brought forth as the revealed word of God a code of health for the blessing of all who would abide its precepts. I think of the billions of dollars that have been saved for better purposes by those who have refrained from the deleterious substances spoken of in this revelation. I think of the pain and the misery they have been spared. I think of the findings of modern science decrying the use of tobacco and alcohol, of caffeine and other substances. I think of the research that clearly indicates added average longevity for those who follow these teachings. I think of the promise of great treasures of knowledge, even hidden treasures. That promise has been fulfilled in a knowledge of the eternal purposes of God revealed unto this people through the great Prophet of this dispensation.

I thank him and love him for the organization of The Church of Jesus Christ of Latter-day Saints. It is a marvel and a miracle under which millions hold office and responsibility in the church and kingdom of God. It is a unique system of ecclesiastical government under which the authority to nominate rests with the presiding officers, but the right to serve is conditioned upon the approval of the membership.

I thank him and the Lord from whom it came for this marvelous organization, which is able to function in any land or society, where leadership comes out of the people, where, with few exceptions, the call to serve is but for a season, thereby ensuring a constant renewal of talent, outlook, energy, and spiritual strength.

I thank the Prophet and love him for the simplicity and effectiveness of the Church law of revenue, which came to him through revelation. People of many nations, and their professional accountants, wrestle with complex tax codes. Contrast this with the wisdom of the Almighty as revealed to His Prophet. The entire code for both obtaining and disbursing the means for the upkeep and program of the Church is found in two short verses: "Those who have . . . been tithed shall pay one-tenth of all their interest annually; and this shall be a standing law unto them forever, for my holy priesthood, saith the Lord" (D&C 119:4).

Such is the law of revenue. If an individual writes to the First Presidency regarding the definition of tithing, as many do, asking about this detail or that, he or she will receive an answer simply referring to section 119 of the Doctrine and Covenants with the only interpretation being that the word "interest" should be interpreted as "income."

As for disbursement of the funds so gathered, the direction is clear and simple and straightforward: "It shall be disposed of by a council, composed of the First Presidency of my Church, and of the bishop and his council, and by my high council; and by mine own voice unto them, saith the Lord. Even so. Amen" (D&C 120).

That is all there is to it. And the marvelous thing is that it works. We are carrying forward a vast and costly program that reaches into scores of nations and political entities. To me, it is a constant miracle what is being done. I am in a position to see this miracle. In all of its ecclesiastical operations scattered across the world, the

Church has no debt. I thank the Lord for the faith of the Latter-day Saints, which makes all of this possible. I love and thank the Prophet Joseph Smith as an instrument through whom the Lord revealed this, so simple and effective, in contrast with the complex methods of men.

I thank him and love him for the sacrifice that he made, giving his life for the cause he loved and sealing his testimony with his blood.

When in June of 1844 he crossed the Mississippi to Montrose to escape his enemies, he told Stephen Markham that if he were taken again he would be "massacred." He was young then, only thirty-eight and a few months. He was at the zenith of his ministry. Nauvoo was then a place of industry and growth. In only five years it had risen from the swamps to become perhaps the most impressive city in all of the state of Illinois. He was loved by his people and, in turn, he loved them. Their numbers were increasing as missionaries spread the word in the eastern United States, Canada, and the British Isles. A magnificent temple was rising on the hill to the east, up the slope from the river. This was the prime time of his life, but there were a few who spoke of cowardice in running away. When he heard this, he said, "If my life is of no value to my friends, it is of none to myself."

He returned to Nauvoo. He was arrested on false charges. As he gazed upon the city while being escorted to Carthage, he said, "This is the loveliest place and the best people under the heavens."

While en route to his rendezvous with death, he said, "I am going like a lamb to the slaughter . . . and it shall . . . be said of me—He was murdered in cold blood" (D&C 135:4).

I love him for the brooding sorrow of those last hours in the old jail. John Taylor sang, "A Poor Wayfaring Man of Grief." Then, at Joseph's request, he sang it again. There was a certain simplicity and sadness in the music and something of comfort, reassurance, and meaning in the words. Then came the vile, cursing, ugly mob. Shots were fired, and the Prophet fell from the window. It was the afternoon of 27 June 1844.

John Taylor, who had been wounded when Joseph and Hyrum were killed, wrote their epitaph:

> Joseph Smith, the Prophet and Seer of the Lord, has done more, save Jesus only, for the salvation of men in this world, than any other man that ever lived in it. In the short space of twenty years, he has brought forth the Book of Mormon, which he translated by the gift and power of God, and has been the means of publishing it on two continents; has sent the fulness of the everlasting gospel, which it contained, to the four quarters of the earth; has brought forth the revelations and commandments which compose this book of Doctrine and Covenants, and many other wise documents and instructions for the benefit of the children of men; gathered many thousands of the Latter-day Saints, founded a great city, and left a fame and name that cannot be slain. He lived great, and he died great in the eyes of God and his people; and like most of the Lord's anointed in ancient times, has sealed his mission and his works with his own blood; and so has his brother Hyrum. In life they were not divided, and in death they were not separated!
>
> . . . From age to age shall their names go down to posterity as gems for the sanctified. (D&C 135:3, 6)

Of the events of that tragic 27 June, Governor Thomas Ford of Illinois wrote, "Thus fell Joe Smith, the most successful imposter in modern times; a man who, though ignorant and coarse, had some great natural parts which fitted him for temporary success, but which were so obscured and counteracted by the inherent corruption and vices of his nature that he never could succeed in establishing a system of policy which looked to permanent success in the future" (*History of Illinois*, 2:213).

The man who wrote that appraisal died six years later, practically bankrupt, leaving five orphaned children to the mercy of others. Both he and his wife, who had died three months earlier, were buried at public expense. He is remembered for little more than his association with the death of the Prophet Joseph.

I like to compare his appraisal with the prophetic statement given by Moroni when he appeared to the boy Joseph the night of 21 September 1823. On that occasion Joseph records that the angel said "that God had a work for me to do; and that my name should be had for good and evil among all nations, kindreds, and tongues, or that it should be both good and evil spoken of among all people" (JS–H 1:33).

And further, I compare Governor Ford's statement with these remarkable words of prophecy given in the cold and misery of Liberty Jail in March of 1839. On that occasion the Lord said to Joseph:

> The ends of the earth shall inquire after thy name, and fools shall have thee in derision, and hell shall rage against thee;
> While the pure in heart, and the wise, and the noble, and the virtuous, shall seek counsel, and authority, and blessings constantly from under thy hand.
> And thy people shall never be turned against thee by the testimony of traitors. (D&C 122:1–3)

The spirit in which Thomas Ford in 1850 wrote his appraisal of the Prophet is evident. The ever-widening fulfillment of the words of Moroni spoken in 1823 and the words of the Lord revealed in 1839 is also evident.

I have walked about the beautiful grounds in Sharon, Windsor County, Vermont, where Joseph was born 23 December 1805. I have looked at the marble shaft thirty-eight and one-half feet high, one foot for each year of his life. I have reflected, in that environment, upon what was started here when mortal life came to one who in the premortal existence was among the noble and great to come to earth and fulfill an appointed mission. Said Brigham Young:

> It was decreed in the counsels of eternity, long before the foundations of the earth were laid, that he [Joseph Smith] should be the man, in the last dispensation of this world, to bring forth the word of God to the people, and receive the fulness of the keys and powers of the Priesthood of the Son of God. The Lord had his eye upon him, and upon his father, and upon his father's father, and upon their progenitors clear back to Abraham, and from Abraham to the flood, from the flood to Enoch, and from Enoch to Adam. He has watched that family and that blood as it has circulated from its fountain to the birth of that man. He was fore-ordained in eternity to preside over this last dispensation. (*Journal of Discourses,* 7:289–90)

I have walked where he walked through the fields to the Sacred Grove. Some years ago in company with the Rochester stake president, the Cumorah mission president, and a Regional Representative, I went to the Sacred Grove early in the morning of a spring Sabbath day. It had been raining in the night. Little drops of water glistened on the tiny new leaves. We prayed together in that quiet and hallowed place, and there came into my heart at that time a conviction that what the Prophet described actually happened in 1820 there amidst the trees.

I have climbed the slopes of the Hill Cumorah. I have walked the banks of the Susquehanna River. I have been to Kirtland, to Independence, Liberty, Far West, Adam-ondi-Ahman, Nauvoo, and Carthage. While I have never met Joseph Smith, I think I have come to know him, at least in some small measure.

I know that he was foreordained to a mighty work to serve as an instrument of the Almighty in bringing to pass a restoration of the work of God of all previous dispensations of time. I have read the Book of Mormon, again and again. I know that he did not write it out of his own capacity. I know that he was a translator who, by the gift and power of God, brought forth this great testament of the new world. I know that it is true, that it is powerful, that it is a witness to the nations of the Divine Redeemer of mankind, the Living Son of the Living God.

I know that the priesthood is upon the earth. I have seen its power. I know that The Church of Jesus Christ of Latter-day Saints is true. I have witnessed again and again the miracle that comes into the lives of men and women who accept it and become part of its inspired program.

I worship the God of heaven, who is my Eternal Father. I worship the Lord Jesus Christ, who is my Savior and my Redeemer. I do not worship the Prophet Joseph Smith, but I reverence and love this great seer through whom the miracle of this gospel has been restored. I am now growing old, and I know that in the natural course of events, before many years, I will step across the threshold to stand before my Maker and my Lord and give an accounting of my life. And I hope that I shall have the opportunity of embracing the Prophet Joseph Smith and of thanking him and of speaking of my love for him.

CHAPTER 2

THE PROPHET JOSEPH SMITH: TEACHER BY EXAMPLE

PRESIDENT THOMAS S. MONSON

"I was born in the year of our Lord one thousand eight hundred and five, on the twenty-third day of December, in the town of Sharon, Windsor county, State of Vermont" (JS–H 1:3). Thus spoke the first prophet of this great dispensation, the dispensation of the fulness of times. These words of the Prophet Joseph Smith and his testimony which follows have been translated into Portuguese, Spanish, Chinese, Russian, German, French, Polish, and almost every other language of the civilized world. When read by honest men and honest women, these profound words have changed thinking and have changed lives. This is the value of the simple testimony of the boy prophet, Joseph Smith.

Let us go back to the year of our Lord 1805, on the twenty-third day of December, in the town of Sharon, Windsor County, Vermont. Will you take that journey with me? Will you accompany me as we look back on those dramatic events taking place on that day? As Joseph Smith, Sr., and his wife, Lucy Mack, proudly looked down upon the little baby that had come into their home, I'm certain they were pleased and most grateful to the Lord that the period of her confinement had passed favorably and that this child had been born to them. I can imagine that they might have exclaimed, as did the poet, that this little baby was "a sweet, new blossom of humanity, fresh fallen from God's own home to flower on earth."[1] A choice spirit had come to dwell in its earthly tabernacle.

Some have asked, "Did he have an unusual childhood or boyhood?" "Was the Prophet Joseph different from me or my brothers?" I think we could perhaps gain insight into the childhood of the Prophet by reading the words of his mother, Lucy. She said, "I am aware that some of my readers will be disappointed, for . . . it is thought by some that I shall be likely to tell many very remarkable incidents which attended his childhood; but, as nothing occurred during his early life except those trivial circumstances which are common to that state of human existence, I pass them in silence."[2] This is all we have from the boy's mother concerning his early childhood activities.

During his early youth, however, ill health and ill fortune seemed to pursue the family. The good father tried farming in several localities but couldn't quite succeed in any of them. When young Joseph was seven years old, he and his brothers and sisters were stricken with typhus fever. The others recovered readily, but Joseph was left with a painful sore on his leg, a sore which would not heal. The doctors, doing the best they could under the conditions of the time, treated him—and yet the sore persisted. Finally the doctors were afraid they were going to have to amputate his leg.

We can imagine the grief and the sorrow that would come to parents who were told that the leg of their young son must be removed. Thankfully, however, one day the doctors came unexpectedly to the home, and they told the family that they were going to try a new operation to remove a piece of the bone, hoping that this would permit the sore to heal. They had brought with them some cord and planned to tie Joseph to the bed because they had no anesthetic, nothing to dull the pain, when they cut into his leg to remove the piece of bone.

Young Joseph, however, responded, "I will not be bound, for I can bear the operation much better if I have my liberty."

The doctors then said, "Will you take some wine? . . . You must take something, or you can never endure the severe operation."

Again the boy prophet said, "No, . . . but I will tell you what I will do—I will have my father sit on the bed and hold me in his arms, and then I will do whatever is necessary in order to have the bone taken out."

So Joseph Smith, Sr., held the boy in his arms, and the doctors opened the leg and removed the diseased piece of bone. Although he was lame for some time afterward, Joseph was healed.[3] At seven years of age, the Prophet Joseph Smith taught us courage—*by example.*

When Joseph was in his tenth year, his family, which now consisted of eleven souls, left the state of Vermont and moved to Palmyra, Ontario County, New York. Four years later they moved to Manchester, located in the same county. It was here that Joseph described the great religious revival which seemed everywhere present and of prime concern to every heart. These are his words: "So great were the confusion and strife among the different denominations, that it was impossible for a person young as I was, and so unacquainted with men and things, to come to any certain conclusion who was right and who was wrong. . . .

"While I was laboring under the extreme difficulties caused by the contests of these parties of religionists, I was one day reading the Epistle of James, first chapter and fifth verse, which reads: *If any of you lack wisdom, let him ask of God, that giveth to all men liberally, and upbraideth not; and it shall be given him*" (JS–H 1:8, 11).

The Prophet said that after reading this verse he knew for a certainty he must either put the Lord to the test and ask Him or perhaps choose to remain in darkness forever. He declared that as he retired to the grove to pray, this was the first time he had attempted to pray vocally to his Heavenly Father. But he had read the scripture, he had understood the scripture, he had trusted in God his Eternal Father; and now he knelt and prayed, knowing that God would give him the enlightenment which he so earnestly sought. The Prophet Joseph Smith taught us the principle of faith—*by example.*

Can you imagine the ridicule, the scorn, the mocking which all of his young friends, his older friends, and his foes alike must have heaped upon him when he declared that he had seen a vision? I suppose that it became almost unbearable for the boy, and yet he was honest with himself, for these are his words: "I had actually seen a light, and in the midst of that light I saw two Personages, and they did in reality speak to me; and though I was hated and persecuted for saying that I had seen a vision, yet it was true; and while they were persecuting me, reviling me, and speaking all manner of evil against me falsely for so saying, I was led to say in my heart: Why persecute me for telling the truth? I have actually seen a vision; and who am I that I can withstand God, or why does the world think to make me deny what I have actually seen? For I had seen a vision; I knew it, and I knew that God knew it, and I could not deny it" (JS–H 1:25). The Prophet Joseph Smith taught honesty—*by example.*

An unusual thing happened after that great first vision. The Prophet Joseph received no additional communication for three years. However, he did not wonder, he did not question, he did not doubt the Lord. The Prophet Joseph patiently waited. The Prophet Joseph taught us the principle of patience—*by example.*

Following the visits of the angel Moroni and the delivering into the hands of the Prophet the golden plates, he commenced the difficult assignment of translation, which would absorb his every waking moment, his every thought, his every action night and day, perhaps every hour. One can but imagine the dedication, the devotion, and the labor required to translate in less than ninety days this record of over five hundred pages, which covered a period of twenty-six hundred years. There is not an absurd, impossible, or contradictory statement in the entire book. Joseph worked, Joseph studied, Joseph applied himself to his task. The Prophet Joseph Smith taught us diligence—*by example.*

I love the words Oliver Cowdery used to describe the time he spent assisting Joseph with the translation: "These were days never to be forgotten—to sit under the sound of a voice dictated by the inspiration of heaven, awakened the utmost gratitude of this bosom! Day after day I continued, uninterrupted, to write from his mouth, as he translated with the Urim and Thummim . . . the history or record called 'The Book of Mormon'" (JS–H, endnote).

The Prophet Joseph was truly blessed with the ability to inspire faith. One bright morning Joseph walked up to John E. Page and said, "Brother John, the Lord is calling you on a mission to Canada."

John E. Page was rather astonished and said, "Why, Brother Joseph, I can't go on a mission to Canada. I don't even have a coat to wear."

The Prophet Joseph took his own coat from his back, handed it to John Page, and said, "Here, John, wear this, and the Lord will bless you." Brother Page took the coat, went to Canada, and in two years walked five thousand miles and baptized six hundred souls, because he trusted in the words of a prophet of God.[4]

On another occasion Joseph was speaking to a group of brethren at Nauvoo on the importance of missionary work, and at the conclusion of his message he had so touched the congregation that 380 elders in the congregation volunteered to immediately embark on missions.[5]

The Prophet Joseph believed in missionary work. While he and Sidney Rigdon were proselyting at Perrysburg, New York, 12 October 1833, having been long absent from their families and feeling concerned for them, they received the following revelation:

> Verily, thus saith the Lord unto you, my friends Sidney and Joseph, your families are well; they are in mine hands, and I will do with them as seemeth me good; for in me there is all power.
>
> Therefore, follow me, and listen to the counsel which I shall give unto you.
>
> Behold, . . . I have much people in this place, in the regions round about; and an effectual door shall be opened in the regions round about in this eastern land. . . .

Therefore, verily I say unto you, lift up your voices unto this people; speak the thoughts that I shall put into your hearts, and you shall not be confounded before men;

For it shall be given you . . . in the very moment, what ye shall say. . . .

And I give unto you this promise, that inasmuch as ye do this the Holy Ghost shall be shed forth in bearing record unto all things whatsoever ye shall say. (D&C 100:1–8)

Joseph and Sidney continued their missionary labors.

Joseph Smith not only inspired men to volunteer for missions, he not only took his own coat and handed it to John Page as he went on his mission, but he also taught the importance of missionary work—*by example.*

I think one of the sweetest lessons taught by the Prophet, and yet one of the saddest, occurred close to the time of his death. He had seen in vision the Saints leaving Nauvoo and going to the Rocky Mountains. I imagine he felt as did Moses—anxious to lead his people away from their tormentors and into a promised land that the Lord his God had shown him. But it was not to be. Rather, he was required to leave his plan and vision of the Rocky Mountains and give himself up to face a court of supposed justice.

These are his words: "I am going like a lamb to the slaughter; but I am calm as a summer's morning; I have a conscience void of offense towards God, and towards all men" (D&C 135:4). That statement of the Prophet teaches us obedience to law and the importance of having a clear conscience toward God and toward our fellowmen. The Prophet Joseph Smith taught these principles—*by example.*

There was to be one great final lesson before his mortal life ended. He was incarcerated in Carthage Jail with his brother Hyrum, with John Taylor, and with Willard Richards. The angry mob stormed the jail; they came up the stairway, blasphemous in their cursing, heavily armed, and began to fire at will. Hyrum was hit and died. John Taylor took several balls of fire within his bosom. The Prophet Joseph, with his pistol in hand, was attempting to defend his life and that of his brethren, and yet he could tell from the pounding on the door that this mob would storm that door and would kill John Taylor and Willard Richards in an attempt to kill him. And so his last great act here upon the earth was to leave the door and lead Willard Richards to safety, throw the gun on the floor, and go to the window, that they might see him, that the attention of this ruthless mob might be focused upon him rather than the others. Joseph Smith gave his life. Willard Richards was spared, and John Taylor recovered from his wounds. "Greater love hath no man than this, that a man lay down his life for his friends" (John 15:13). The Prophet Joseph Smith taught us love—*by example.*

Joseph Smith, the first prophet of this dispensation, sealed his testimony of the Restoration with his blood. I testify that he was a prophet of God. I have seen the Lord convert people to His plan of salvation through the testimony of the Prophet Joseph. Many years ago, when I became president of the Canadian Mission, headquartered in Toronto, Canada, one of the first accounts I heard was of the conversion of Elmer Pollard. Two missionaries had been proselyting door to door on a cold, snowy afternoon. They had not experienced any measure of success. One had been in the mission field for some time; one was a newly arrived missionary.

The two missionaries called at the home of Elmer Pollard. Feeling sorry for the young men who, during a blinding blizzard were going house to house, Mr. Pollard invited the missionaries into his home. They presented their message to him. He did not catch the spirit. In due time he asked that they leave and not return. His last words to the elders as they departed his front porch were spoken in derision: "You can't tell me you actually believe Joseph Smith was a prophet of God!"

The door was shut; the elders walked down the path. The newly arrived missionary spoke to his companion, "Elder, we didn't respond to Mr. Pollard. He said we didn't believe Joseph Smith was a true prophet. Let's return and bear our testimonies to him."

At first the more experienced missionary was adamant about not returning, but finally he agreed to accompany his "green" companion. Fear struck their hearts as they approached the door from which they had been turned away. Then came the knock, the confrontation with Mr. Pollard, an agonizing moment—and then, with power, a testimony borne by the Spirit. "Mr. Pollard," began the new missionary, "you said we didn't really believe Joseph Smith was a prophet of God. Mr. Pollard, I testify that Joseph Smith was a prophet; he did translate the Book of Mormon; he saw God the Father and Jesus the Son. I know it."

Mr. Pollard, now Brother Pollard, stood in a priesthood meeting some time later and declared, "That night I could not sleep. Resounding in my ears I heard the words, 'Joseph Smith was a prophet of God. I know it. I know it.' The next day I telephoned the missionaries. Their message, coupled with their testimonies, changed my life and the lives of my family."

In the 135th section of the Doctrine and Covenants we read the words of John Taylor concerning the Prophet Joseph:

> Joseph Smith, the Prophet and Seer of the Lord, has done more, save Jesus only, for the salvation of men in this world, than any other man that ever lived in it. In the short space of twenty years, he has brought forth the Book of Mormon, which he translated by the gift and power of God, and has been the means of publishing it on two continents; has sent the fulness of the everlasting gospel, which it contained, to the four quarters of the earth; has brought forth the revelations and commandments which compose this book of Doctrine and Covenants, and many other wise documents and instructions . . . ; gathered many thousands of the Latter-day Saints, founded a great city, and left a fame and name that cannot be slain. He lived great, and he died great in the eyes of God and his people; and like most of the Lord's anointed in ancient times, has sealed his mission and his works with his own blood. (D&C 135:3)

What a fitting tribute to a prophet of God! I pray we may learn from his example, that we might incorporate into our lives the great principles which he so beautifully taught; that we ourselves might emulate him; that our lives might reflect the knowledge we have that God lives, that Jesus is His Son, and that we are led today by a prophet of God.

NOTES

1. Gerald Massey.
2. Lucy Mack Smith, *History of Joseph Smith*, ed. Preston Nibley (Salt Lake City: Bookcraft, 1979), p. 67.
3. See ibid., pp. 54–58.
4. See *Historical Record 5*, no. 5 (May 1886): 57.
5. See *History of the Church*, 5:139.

THE EXPANDING INHERITANCE FROM JOSEPH SMITH

PRESIDENT JAMES E. FAUST

It was Friday morning, 28 June 1844, and already the summer sun was hot in Illinois. Since about eight o'clock that morning, Dr. Willard Richards, Samuel H. Smith, and nine others had plodded along the dusty road between Carthage and Nauvoo, Illinois. Moving along the road with the solemn procession were two wagons heaped with bushes to protect their cargo from the blistering heat of the sun.

Laid out on the wagons were the lifeless bodies of Joseph Smith, age thirty-eight, over six feet tall, and Hyrum, his brother, age forty-four, and even larger in stature than Joseph. Wearily, Dr. Richards and Samuel Smith, brother to the two murdered men, pressed toward Nauvoo and talked of the events just the day before, during which Joseph and Hyrum were gunned down by an armed mob with painted faces. The two victims, along with Dr. Richards and John Taylor, were lodged in Carthage Jail, supposedly for their protection, when the mob, numbering from 150 to 200 marauders, stormed the jail and shot to death their intended victims.

Word of the deaths had already reached Nauvoo, headquarters city for The Church of Jesus Christ of Latter-day Saints. As the wagons and their foot-weary guardians entered the city, several thousand citizens greeted the procession with the most solemn lamentations and mourning.

The bloodied bodies were tenderly removed from the wagons at the Nauvoo Mansion and were carefully washed from head to foot. The various wounds were filled with cotton, soaked in camphor, and death masks were impressed on each face. Fine, plain clothing was then placed on each body. When these preparations were completed, the bodies were viewed that night by the bereaved widows and children of the two men, along with many of their closest associates. Then on Saturday, more than ten thousand mourning Saints viewed the remains of their beloved Prophet Joseph and his brother, the Patriarch Hyrum. The bodies were then secretly and lovingly buried.[1]

Some of the enemies of Joseph Smith exulted in their infamous deeds; and many proclaimed that the Church, which he had restored and for which he had given his life, would die with him.

But, to the surprise of its enemies, the Church did not die nor did the work of Joseph Smith cease with his mortal death. What has transpired in a century and a half bears eloquent testimony to the eternal nature of the work of this singularly remarkable man, Joseph Smith. The Church which he restored has had dramatic growth in many parts of the earth. It has produced an unequaled missionary system and an unmatched welfare program. Its governing system gives priesthood power and authority from God to all worthy male members, at the same time recognizing the exalted status of women as being equal to men. The Church has an inspired law of health and temporal well-being far ahead of its time. By revelation from God, the Church also possesses those keys, saving principles, and ordinances which will bring eternal exaltation to mankind, living and dead.

Because of these and other reasons, millions of people have become members of The Church of Jesus Christ of Latter-day Saints. But to each true believer there must ultimately and finally come a conviction that Joseph Smith was a revealer of truth, a prophet of God. Each must be convinced that God the Father and his Son Jesus Christ did appear to Joseph Smith and did commission him to reestablish the church of Christ upon the face of the earth.

I have such a conviction, and it is my humble desire to share with you some of the things that verify my testimony of Joseph Smith and his work. My own witness is a spiritual one more than a scientific or historical one. I doubt that the gospel of Jesus Christ as restored to earth through the Prophet Joseph Smith, and as taught by all the prophets who have succeeded him, will ever be completely provable by the scientific method alone. It must be accepted by faith and understood by the gift and power of God. For instance, one of the truths revealed by Joseph Smith, on 27 February 1833, taught of the harmful effects of tea, coffee, tobacco, and alcoholic beverages. Such teachings today can be proven scientifically, yet in my opinion, the greatest promises contained in the Word of Wisdom (D&C 89) are spiritual. It contains a promise of wisdom and great treasures of knowledge, and of the passing by of the destroying angel as the children of Israel were passed by (see D&C 89:19, 21).

One of the most significant contributions of Joseph Smith is his work in translating and publishing the Book of Mormon, a sacred volume of scripture brought forth from ancient records. When it was first published in 1830, there was little scientific or historical evidence to substantiate the claims of Joseph Smith that the record came from metallic plates and told of ancient civilizations on the North and South American continents. Today such outward evidences have been discovered and help confirm that Joseph Smith was telling the truth about the Book of Mormon.

But we also still look to the spiritual witnesses for our confirming belief in the book. Critics have long tried to explain away the Book of Mormon but simply have not been successful. Theories concerning its origin have come and gone, and the book still lives on to testify that Jesus is the Christ.

Most objective, analytical scholars have come to recognize that it would have been impossible for an uneducated boy such as Joseph Smith, reared on the frontiers of America, to write the Book of Mormon. It contains so many exalted concepts, has such different writing styles, and is compiled in such a way that no one person could be its author. The honest inquirer can be led by faith to believe that Joseph Smith did translate the Book of Mormon from ancient plates of gold that were written with engraved characters in the reformed Egyptian language. No other explanations that have seriously challenged Joseph Smith's own account of the Book of Mormon have been able to survive as being factually correct. The evidences of a century and a half continue, and these increasingly affirm that Joseph Smith spoke the truth, completely, honestly, and humbly.

As I submit to you my testimony of Joseph Smith, I acknowledge his humanness along with his great spiritual powers. He did not claim to be divine, nor a perfect man. He claimed only to be a mortal man with human feelings and imperfections, trying honestly to fulfill the divine mission given to him. He so describes himself in recorded counsel given to some of the members of the Church who had just arrived in Nauvoo on 29 October 1842. Said the Prophet, "I told them I was but a man, and they must not expect me to be perfect; if they expected perfection from me, I should expect it from them; but if they would bear with my infirmities and the infirmities of the brethren, I would likewise bear with their infirmities."[2]

I am impressed with his complete candor, for in addition to admitting his own humanness, he also recorded the declarations from the Lord that were given to him in the nature of loving reproof. As such reminders came to him, sometimes kindly and sometimes sternly, he dictated them as the mouthpiece of the Lord to those who transcribed the revelations. One such example is found in the Doctrine and Covenants, section five, verse twenty-one: "And now I command you, my servant Joseph, to repent and walk more uprightly before me, and to yield to the persuasions of men no more."

While Joseph sought perfection, he did not claim perfection. If he were intending to fabricate a great falsehood or wanted to perpetrate a fraud or practice deceit, would he have been so truthful about his own humanness? His complete candor in admitting human frailties and in declaring the loving discipline of God offers powerful proof of his honesty and probity. His statements stand on more solid footing because they were declarations against human nature and admissions against self-interest.

He knew that such candor would and did make him an object of hatred, ridicule, and social disapproval, but he spoke openly the unvarnished truth. He was prepared for such vicissitudes of life early in his ministry. He was told by the angel Moroni in 1823, only three years after his glorious vision of God the Father and Jesus Christ, that his name would be known for good and evil among all nations, kindreds, tongues, and peoples, and that both good and evil would be spoken of him (see JS–H 1:33). However, the intensity of the evil and persecution surprised even Joseph and caused him to ask on one occasion: "Why should the powers of darkness combine against me? Why the opposition and persecution that arose against me, almost in my infancy?" (JS–H 1:20). But he met the challenges and overcame the strife and was stronger because of them.

There should be no exaggerated emphasis on the fallibility or mortal failings of Joseph Smith. They were only things that are a part of any human being. He and his work enjoyed the benediction of Deity. On a special occasion, the Lord said to him: "Verily, thus saith the Lord unto you, my servant Joseph Smith, I am well pleased with your offering and acknowledgments, which you have made; for unto this end have I raised you up, that I might show forth my wisdom through the weak things of the earth" (D&C 124:1).

I am deeply impressed by the kinds of people who became associates of Joseph Smith. His personality was a magnet to many people, attracting those of all ages and all classes. Many whom he inspired were extremely intelligent, dedicated, and capable men and women. The courage that they evidenced in behalf of the work of

Joseph Smith, as well as their sacrifices, suffering, and dedication, was almost beyond belief.

At the outset I mentioned Dr. Willard Richards, whose loyalty to Joseph is so typical. Before Joseph went to Carthage Jail, he said to Dr. Richards: "'If we go into the cell, will you go in with us?' The doctor answered, 'Brother Joseph you did not ask me to cross the river with you—you did not ask me to come to Carthage—you did not ask me to come to jail with you—and do you think I would forsake you now? But I will tell you what I will do; if you are condemned to be hung for treason, I will be hung in your stead, and you shall go free.' Joseph said, 'You cannot.' The doctor replied, 'I will.'"[3]

Following the martyrdom of Joseph Smith, his successor as prophet was the practical, able Brigham Young. Of Joseph Smith, Brigham Young said:

"When I first heard him preach, he brought heaven and earth together; and all the priests of the day could not tell me anything correct about heaven, hell, God, angels, or devils; they were as blind as Egyptian darkness. When I saw Joseph Smith, he took heaven, figuratively speaking, and brought it down to earth; and he took the earth, brought it up, and opened up, in plainness and simplicity, the things of God; and that is the beauty of his mission."[4]

The results of a century and a half of this church offer great authentication to the truthfulness of Joseph Smith's story. The work of this church moves forward in an astonishing way. The great body of the Latter-day Saints remain faithful to their testimonies of Joseph Smith and his work. Since Joseph's day, millions have accepted by faith and have had confirmed by the Holy Spirit that Joseph's account of seeing the Father and the Son is true and that he restored to earth the pure gospel of Jesus Christ.

As the years pass since Joseph's life and death, his history will no doubt be analyzed, picked at, criticized, challenged, and pored over. But the evidences of the truthfulness of his statements will continue to mount. The devotion and commitment of those who accept the restored gospel will continue to be severely tested. Their faith will be sorely tried, as has been the case with so many in the past. But like Joseph himself, millions will live and die faithful to the gospel he restored. As time moves on, the stature of Joseph Smith will loom ever larger. He will stand higher and higher in the esteem of mankind. Ever so many will come to a profound conviction, as I have, that there is a divine source to the message he taught and an eternal purpose to the work which he restored on earth.

There comes down through my family a legacy of testimony concerning the truthfulness of Joseph Smith's work. I learned of this bequest as a small boy at my mother's knee. My great-great-grandfather, Edward Partridge, was intimately associated with the Prophet Joseph for several years prior to losing his life in consequence of persecution.[5] He was baptized by Joseph. In a revelation received by the Prophet, he was called as the first bishop of the restored Church (see D&C 41:9).

Grandfather was so tortured and humiliated, and suffered so much in his calling from lawless mobs, yet was still so steadfast and faithful, that he could not possibly have doubted the genuineness of the revelation that appointed him. Like others who were close to the Prophet, he knew Joseph's heart and soul. Grandfather could not have been deceived. I believe his life and death both prove that he did not lie. His devotion, suffering, and sacrifice eloquently testify that he had implicit faith in Joseph as an inspired servant of God.

In addition to this heritage, I have my own inner witness which confirms to my soul that the Prophet Joseph Smith, as the instrument of God, revealed the greatest body of truth that has come to mankind since the Savior himself walked upon the earth.

What current prophets and apostles teach us is an extension of the expanding inheritance of truth left to all of us by the Prophet Joseph Smith. It was given to save and exalt mankind as directed by the Lord Jesus Christ. I so testify with profound gratitude.

NOTES

1. See *History of the Church,* 6:614–31.
2. Ibid., 5:181.
3. Ibid., 6:616.
4. *Discourses of Brigham Young,* sel. John A. Widtsoe (Salt Lake City: Deseret Book Co., 1954), p. 458.
5. See *History of the Church,* 4:132.

JOSEPH SMITH THE PROPHET

ELDER DAVID B. HAIGHT

CHAPTER

4

The eternal truths of the gospel are being accepted by an ever-growing body of believers throughout the world. The work of our local Church members, in harmony with that of our full-time missionaries, is resulting in a rapid expansion of this Church.

In 1979, it was my privilege to be assigned to create new stakes in Lima, Peru. We met in a coliseum with over seven thousand Saints and investigators. After this moving spiritual experience, we were confronted by three newspaper reporters in the parking lot. They asked: "Why are you in Lima?" "How many members does your church have in Peru?" "Why is your church growing so rapidly?" "What are your church's future plans?"

And then a young woman reporter asked, "What is the difference between your church and other churches?"

The crowd was large and pressing toward us, the traffic rather noisy. We were on a close time schedule. It was not an ideal setting, not one I would have chosen to explain the difference between the Lord's church and others. However, taking advantage of this opportunity, we explained briefly the Apostasy and the Restoration: that there is vast evidence and history of an apostasy from the doctrine taught by Jesus and his apostles, that the organization of the original Church became corrupted and sacred ordinances were changed to suit the convenience of men, and that today good people all over the world are confused with contending religions with differing doctrine and methods of worship.

The reporters listened intently. We explained to them that after a long period of darkness there was a heavenly directed restoration of the true gospel of the Savior, that a young man named Joseph Smith was chosen and schooled to be the instrument to perform the foundation labor for the marvelous work which God has established as his church in these last days.

As we briefly told of the Restoration and of Joseph Smith, his profile focused in my mind in a most interesting way. It was an unusual experience. As the Prophet's facial profile remained in my mind, I thought: "If these reporters and the world could only understand the entire story and the significance of the Restoration—of the eternal blessings God has made available to all. If they could only feel as I feel. If they could know, as I know, if they could only realize the calling and the role of the Prophet."

I added my witness that Joseph Smith was divinely commissioned as the restorer of the gospel of Jesus Christ in its fulness, that he was and is a prophet of God, that he sought God in prayer and God spoke to him. He did the work Jesus, the Son of God, commanded him to do, and this Church, which the Prophet assisted in organizing, is possessor of the divine keys and authority of the holy priesthood, and is charged with the responsibility to carry God's plan of salvation to all his earthly children.

Man was wondering then as now: "Is there a God? Can he speak to man? Is he concerned with individual human needs?"

A young man not unfamiliar with praying, and responding to his youthful faith, entered a grove and, looking around and finding himself alone, kneeled, and offered up the desires of his heart to God. The grove became exceedingly light, brighter than he had ever known. Before him stood two glorious personages—defying all description. One pointed to the other and said, *"This is My Beloved Son. Hear Him!"* The Son spoke to the kneeling boy. Joseph was told that all the churches were wrong—they had corrupted the doctrine, had changed the ordinances, and had lost the authority of the priesthood—and that he, unlearned but humble, was to be the instrument through whom the Almighty would reestablish his work (see JS–H 1:15–20).

The prevalent religious teachings of the world had reduced God, in the minds of people, to a fragile spirit, spread throughout the universe, nowhere yet everywhere present—nebulous theories and uncertain doctrine as to the personality of God and the Godhead. Truth had become perverted. When the boy prophet came out of the grove, he had no doubts—he knew. He had looked upon the Father and the Son. They had visited him and instructed him. In the Prophet's own words: "I had seen a vision; I knew it, and I knew that God knew it, and I could not deny it" (JS–H 1:25).

Joseph now knew God is in the form of a man. He has a voice, he speaks, he is kind, he answers prayers. His

Son is like the Father—but a separate and distinct person. Joseph learned the Son is obedient to the Father and mediator between God and man.

The Lord needed a man of steel, one fearless to withstand ridicule and social and political pressures, one like unto Moses, yet greater.

In due course the boy prophet had other angelic visitations. Joseph Smith's account of the coming forth of the Book of Mormon, attended by heavenly messengers, is in full harmony with the appearance of God himself to the Prophet.

The Book of Mormon, a record of the inhabitants of ancient America, was translated "by the gift and power of God" and made available to all people. Its pages are for "the convincing of the Jew and Gentile that Jesus is the Christ, the Eternal God, manifesting himself unto all nations" (Book of Mormon, title page). The Book of Mormon is the most correct book on earth and contains the pure gospel of Christ. It is the most precious book possessed by man.

During the eventful years from the time of the First Vision in 1820 to the June morning of 1844 when two wagons bearing the bodies of Joseph and Hyrum Smith slowly made the six-hour trek from Carthage to Nauvoo, the heavens had opened; the foundation of this great work and kingdom in this dispensation had been laid. The Church of Jesus Christ was organized as anciently. Apostles now held the necessary keys of the priesthood. Joseph's work was done. There never was doubt in his mind or his loyal associates' as to his divine calling, for he had made clear to them his inspired pronouncements.

The organization and priesthood of Christ's original church is restored with apostles, prophets, evangelists, seventies, elders, bishops, priests, teachers, and deacons—

all necessary for the gospel to be preached to every nation and to strengthen members and bind them to the body of Saints.

The Church of Christ is reestablished with doctrine, ordinances, and authority as commissioned by the Savior when he was on the earth. Once again man is ordained with power and authority to carry out His purposes. Uncertainty is removed, the Savior's church and work restored. The doctrine of the restored gospel is comprehensive and complete. It teaches that *"man was . . . in the beginning with God"* (D&C 93:29; emphasis added). That is, man lived before he came to this earth. He is an eternal being. Joseph Smith gave to the world the true understanding of the origin of man, that man comes to earth with a divine and eternal purpose.

Joseph Smith's inspired contributions to all of God's children of the true meaning of life and the destiny of man unfolded little by little, line upon line, through the ministration of angels and others whom the Lord called to the work. The entire account was so glorious and so unexpected that most people of that day could not accept it.

Revelations to Joseph Smith expand man's knowledge that Jesus Christ was crucified to save the world from sin, that through his act of redemption all mankind will be resurrected from the grave and given the possibility of eternal life if obedient to gospel principles.

We are given further enlightenment on Jesus' statement "In my Father's house are many mansions" (John 14:2). We learn not only of the degrees of glory and those eligible to obtain them, but that man should strive for the highest "heaven" which is available, and is reachable only through obedience to all of God's commandments.

President George Albert Smith said: "One of the beautiful things to me in the Gospel of Jesus Christ is that it brings us all to a common level. It is not necessary for a man to be a president of a stake, or a member of the Quorum of the Twelve, in order to attain a high place in the celestial kingdom. The humblest member of the Church, if he keeps the commandments of God, will obtain an exaltation just as much as any other man in the celestial kingdom. The beauty of the Gospel of Jesus Christ is that it makes us all equal. . . . As we keep the commandments of the Lord . . . we have equal opportunities for exaltation" (Conference Report, October 1933, p. 25).

One of the most profound principles of God's love for his children was revealed to Joseph Smith in the Kirtland Temple in 1836. In a vision he saw someone who had not received an opportunity to accept the gospel while living. A voice declared that all who have died without an opportunity to hear the gospel and accept it while on this earth will have the privilege in the spirit world. If they would have received it, given the opportunity, they will be heirs of the celestial kingdom. The Lord "will judge all men according to their works, according to the desire of their hearts" (D&C 137:9).

"Joseph Smith, the Prophet and Seer of the Lord," wrote President John Taylor, "has done more, save Jesus only, for the salvation of men in this world, than any other man that ever lived in it. In the short space of twenty years, he has brought forth the Book of Mormon, which he translated by the gift and power of God, and has been the means of publishing it on two continents; has sent the fulness of the everlasting gospel, which it contained, to the four quarters of the earth; has brought forth the revelations and commandments which compose this book of Doctrine and Covenants, and many other wise documents and instructions for the benefit of the children of men; gathered many thousands of the Latter-day Saints, founded a great city, and left a fame and name that cannot be slain. He lived great, and he died great in the eyes of God and his people; and like most of the Lord's anointed in ancient times, has sealed his mission and his works with his own blood" (D&C 135:3).

While the Saints were still mourning their loss, William W. Phelps, a loyal associate, expressed their feelings when he wrote:

> Praise to the man who communed with Jehovah!
> Jesus anointed that Prophet and Seer.
> Blessed to open the last dispensation,
> Kings shall extol him, and nations revere.
>
> .   .   .   .
>
> Great is his glory and endless his priesthood.
> Ever and ever the keys he will hold.
> Faithful and true, he will enter his kingdom,
> Crowned in the midst of the prophets of old.
> (*Hymns*, 1985, no. 27)

Now, the final restoration has taken place, I testify to you—the restoration of all things "which God hath spoken by the mouth of all his holy prophets since the world began" has been accomplished (Acts 3:21).

The gifts of the Spirit, signs that the gospel has been restored, are with the true Saints.

The gift of the Holy Ghost, through whose power and influence men learn the truth and knowledge of the plan of salvation, is available.

Temples have been built where the Lord may come "and restore again that which was lost . . . , even the fulness of the priesthood" (D&C 124:28).

The Lord himself testified of the Prophet Joseph Smith as He gave a revelation to the Saints at Winter Quarters in January of 1847. He said:

> Marvel not at these things, . . . but ye shall behold it if ye are faithful in keeping all my words that I have given . . . to Joseph Smith, whom I did call upon by mine angels . . . and by mine own voice out of the heavens, to bring forth my work;
>
> Which foundation he did lay, and was faithful; and I took him to myself. (D&C 136:37–38)

Joseph was the prophet of the Restoration. I testify of the divinity of his mission and of his greatness.

JOSEPH, THE SEER

ELDER NEAL A. MAXWELL

Throughout the expanse of human history, no prophet has been scrutinized in such an intense way, on as wide a scale, or for so long a period of time as Joseph Smith, Jr. The communication capacity of this age and the global impact of his work have so ensured.

Young Joseph was told that his name would be "both good and evil spoken of" throughout the world (JS–H 1:33). Except from a divine source, how audacious a statement! Yet his contemporary religious leaders, then much better known than Joseph, have faded into the footnotes of history, while the work of Joseph Smith grows constantly and globally.

We have no hesitancy, however, in stipulating that Joseph was, by the standards of the world, "not learned." Isaiah foresaw it (see Isaiah 29:11–12). Joseph did not have the skilled, formal tutoring young Saul had at the feet of Gamaliel (see Acts 22:3).

Emma Smith reportedly said that Joseph, at the time of the translation of the Book of Mormon, could not compose a "well-worded letter let alone dictating a book like the Book of Mormon . . . [which was] marvelous to me, a marvel and a wonder, as much as to anyone else."[1]

This obscure young man apparently paused while translating and dictating to Emma—probably from the fourth chapter of 1 Nephi—concerning the "walls of Jerusalem"—and said, in effect, to affirming Emma, that he had not known there was a wall around Jerusalem.

But Joseph's keen mind was being awakened and expanded as the tutoring words of the Lord and of past prophets flowed through his quickened consciousness. In fact, he was the very seer foreseen anciently by the earlier Joseph in Egypt! (see 2 Nephi 3:6–7, 14–15).

In a prophetic father's blessing given in December 1834 to Joseph Smith, Jr., Father Smith confirmed those promises given the ancient Joseph, and pronounced added blessings, including these, upon young Joseph: "Thy God has called thee by name out of the heavens . . . to do a work in this generation which no other man would do as Thyself." The ancient Joseph "looked after his posterity in the last days . . . And sought diligently to know . . . who would bring the word of the Lord [to them] and his eyes beheld thee, my son [Joseph Smith, Jr.]: his heart rejoiced and his soul was satisfied."

Young Joseph also heard his father promise, "Thou shalt like to do the work which the Lord shall command Thee" (2 Nephi 3:8).

Earlier, during the approximately seventy-five days of translating, Joseph was processing—and at a remarkable rate—truths and concepts of immense significance, beyond what was then his capacity. A few gems only from that treasure trove:

Could Joseph have been expected, for instance, to appreciate fully that, through him, would be given the only significant scriptural elaboration of one of the most fundamental and demanding declarations of Jesus?

"Verily I say unto you, Except ye be converted, and become as little children, ye shall not enter into the kingdom of heaven" (Matthew 18:3).

Through Joseph Smith's translation came these stunning, defining, and sobering words about what childlike and saintly submissiveness really means:

"A saint [is one who becomes] through the atonement of Christ the Lord . . . a child, submissive, meek, humble, patient, full of love, willing to submit to all things which the Lord seeth fit to inflict upon him, even as a child doth submit to his father" (Mosiah 3:19).

Likewise, Paul wrote that since Jesus was tempted, he understood how to succor us when we are tempted (see Hebrews 2:18; 4:15). Yet it was through Joseph Smith that these confirming and clarifying words of Alma were given:

"And [Jesus] shall go forth, suffering pains and afflictions and temptations of every kind; . . . he will take upon him the pains and the sicknesses of his people. . . . that his bowels may be filled with mercy, according to the flesh, that he may know according to the flesh how to succor his people according to their infirmities" (Alma 7:11–12).

Illuminated also was petitionary prayer: "Whatsoever ye shall ask in prayer, believing, ye shall receive" (Matthew 21:22). "Plain and precious" and needed light was added to those words through Joseph:

"And whatsoever ye shall ask the Father in my name, *which is right*, believing that ye shall receive, behold it shall be given unto you" (3 Nephi 18:20; emphasis added).

"He that asketh in the Spirit asketh according to the will of God; wherefore it is done even as he asketh" (D&C 46:30).

Not only did confirming and clarifying truths flow through Joseph, but also rich language and deep concepts.

From Ammon:

"How blind and impenetrable are the understandings of the children of men; for they will not seek wisdom, neither do they desire that she should rule over them!

"Yea, they are as a wild flock which fleeth from the shepherd, and scattereth, and are driven" (Mosiah 8:20–21).

From Jacob:

"Ye have broken the hearts of your tender wives, and lost the confidence of your children, because of your bad examples before them; . . . many hearts died, pierced with deep wounds" (Jacob 2:35).

From Amulek, who finally triumphed over ambivalence:

"Nevertheless, I did harden my heart, for I was called many times and I would not hear; therefore I knew concerning these things, yet I would not know" (Alma 10:6).

Theology and beauty combine, again and again, in the pages provided through Joseph, as when the resurrected Christ appeared in the Western Hemisphere:

"And when [Jesus] had said these words, he himself also knelt upon the earth; and behold he prayed unto the Father, and the things which he prayed cannot be written. . . .

"And no tongue can speak, neither can there be written by any man, neither can the hearts of men conceive so great and marvelous things as we both saw and heard

Jesus speak; and no one can conceive of the joy which filled our souls at the time we heard him pray for us unto the Father" (3 Nephi 17:15, 17).

Serious study of the blessed Book of Mormon admits one to a wonder world of complexity and beauty, even in the midst of the book's simple, but powerful, spiritual refrain. We are given that which we most need—yet we are athirst for more!

Granted, whenever the words of heaven are filtered through mortal minds and tongues there can be some diminution. Yet, as with Nephi of old, so it was with Joseph Smith:

"If ye shall believe in Christ ye will believe in these words, for they are the words of Christ, and he hath given them unto me" (2 Nephi 33:10).

Joseph later learned to express his own thoughts inspirationally, as in his forgiving letter of 1840 to a betraying but repenting W. W. Phelps.

> It is true, that we have suffered much in consequence of your behavior—the cup of gall, already full enough for mortals to drink, was indeed filled to overflowing when you turned against us. One with whom we had oft taken sweet counsel together, and enjoyed many refreshing seasons from the Lord—"had it been an enemy, we could have borne it." . . .
>
> However, the cup has been drunk, the will of our Father has been done, and we are yet alive, for which we thank the Lord. . . .
>
> . . . I shall be happy once again to . . . rejoice over the returning prodigal. . . .
>
> > "Come on, dear brother, since the war is past,
> > For friends at first, are friends again at last."[2]

Was Joseph imperfect like other prophets? Of course! Surely, Joseph could identify with these words of an ancient prophet, which he translated:

"Condemn me not because of mine imperfection, neither my father, because of his imperfection, . . . but rather give thanks unto God that he hath made manifest unto you our imperfections, that ye may learn to be more wise than we have been" (Mormon 9:31; see also D&C 67:5).

Joseph, who translated the instructive words there is "an opposition in all things" (2 Nephi 2:11), came to understand, by experience, that the calisthenics of spiritual growth involve isometrics, the pitting of the emerging self against the stern resistance of the old self.

Did Joseph experience the same anxieties in carrying out his mission as did other prophets? Indeed! Joseph could understand with what feelings a weary and beset Paul wrote:

"For, when we were come into Macedonia, our flesh had no rest, but we were troubled on every side; without were fightings, within were fears" (2 Corinthians 7:5; see also 2 Corinthians 4:8).

Was Joseph unjustly accused as were other prophets? Yes! Even unto this very day fragments of fact are flung at his memory. Paul was accused of being mad and deranged (see Acts 26:24). Even Jesus himself was accused of being a winebibber, of being possessed of a devil, and of being mad (see Matthew 11:19; John 10:20).

Yet, in the midst of all these things, as promised, Joseph loved the work to which he had been called. And he loved his associates! In giving individual assignments to the Twelve, we see his love and humor tenderly intertwined:

"John Taylor, I believe you can do more good in the editorial department than preaching. You can write for thousands to read; while you can preach to but a few at a time. We have no one else we can trust the paper with, and hardly with you, for you suffer the paper to come out with so many mistakes."[3]

Joseph was filled with mercy, as evidenced in the healing of the many fevered sick on the banks of a river, and where his hands could not go, Joseph sent a healing handkerchief![4]

He sorrowed over his loss of a newborn child and was given permission to care for a neighbor's child during the day, then return the baby to her mother at night. An older sister of the baby, Margarette McIntire, later reported:

"One evening he did not come [home] with [the child] at the usual time, and mother went down to the Mansion to see what was the matter, and there sat the Prophet with the baby wrapped up in a little silk quilt. He was trotting it on his knee, and singing to it to get it quiet before starting out."[5]

Was Joseph a leader-servant? Demonstrably! A girl and her brother were struggling in the deep mud on their way to school. The Prophet Joseph "stooped down and cleaned the mud from our little, heavy-laden shoes, took his handkerchief from his pocket, and wiped our tear-stained faces. He spoke kind and cheering words to us, and sent us on our way to school rejoicing."[6]

In fleeing with Joseph from a mob, a young man reported: "Sickness and fright had robbed me of strength. Joseph had to decide wither to leave me to be captured by the mob or to endanger himself by rendering aid. Choosing the latter course, he lifted me upon his own broad shoulders and bore me with occasional rests through the swamp and darkness. Several hours later we emerged upon the lonely road and soon reached safety. Joseph's herculean strength permitted him to [save] my life."[7]

A victim of intolerance, Joseph Smith was deeply offended when a Catholic convent was burned in New England, saying, "Yes, in sight of the very spot where the fire of American Independence was first kindled."[8] Maligned, even today, Joseph once declared, "I am just as ready to die in defending the rights of a Presbyterian, a Baptist, or . . . any other denomination."[9]

While most mortals misunderstand the significance of Joseph's ministry, the adversary surely did not!

Unsurprisingly, Joseph Smith, Jr., was still growing, spiritually and intellectually, when he was murdered. Yet Joseph lived long enough to "lay out the plan of all the work which God has given you to do" as promised in the blessing from his dying father in 1840. Now the ends of the earth inquire after his name. No wonder an admiring but dying Brigham Young's last words were "Joseph, Joseph, Joseph!"[10]

Thus, those who revile Joseph Smith will not change Joseph's status with the Lord (see 2 Nephi 3:8)—merely their own! Instead—as was promised Joseph in an 1834 father's blessing:

"Thousands and tens of thousands shall come to a knowledge of the truth, through thy ministry, and thou shalt rejoice with Them in the Celestial Kingdom; [and] thou shalt stand on Mount Zion when the tribes of Jacob come shouting from the north, and with thy brethren, the Sons of Ephraim, crown them in the name of Jesus Christ."

Some may seek to explain Joseph merely by attaching to him the generous adjective *remarkable.* Joseph was remarkable, but, much more importantly, he was instrumental!

Even now, one hears faintly the distant but approaching drum roll of history building towards a crescendo of mortal recognition when all shall see "things as they really are" (Jacob 4:13).

Meanwhile, the ancient records that a young Joseph translated will be with us "from generation to generation as long as the earth shall stand" (2 Nephi 25:22; see also D&C 5:10). These very records defined a seer as one who can translate ancient records, who is a revelator, and who knows of things past and future (see Mosiah 8:13–17). Such a seer, wrote Ammon, is greater than a prophet! (see Mosiah 8:15–16). I salute Joseph, the seer!

NOTES

1. Preston Nibley, *The Witnesses of the Book of Mormon* (Salt Lake City: Deseret Book Co., 1968), p. 28.
2. *History of the Church*, 4:163–64.
3. Ibid., 5:367.
4. See ibid., 4:3–5.
5. Quoted in Leonard J. Arrington, "The Human Qualities of Joseph Smith, the Prophet," *Ensign*, Jan. 1971, pp. 36–37.
6. Quoted in "Recollections of the Prophet Joseph Smith," *Juvenile Instructor*, 15 Jan. 1892, p. 67.
7. John L. Smith, quoted in Carl Arrington, "Brother Joseph," *New Era*, Dec. 1973, p. 19.
8. *History of the Church*, 2:465.
9. Ibid., 5:498.
10. Joseph Fielding Smith, *Essentials in Church History*, 24th ed. (Salt Lake City: Deseret Book Co., 1971), p. 459.

chapter 6

AT THE HEART OF THE CHURCH

ELDER RUSSELL M. NELSON

For more than a quarter of a century I have been in the daily practice of "getting to the heart" of the matter. Even though my present calling has taken me out of the surgical operating room, the habit still seems to persist.

I would like to discuss a topic that is at the very heart of our religion. Central to our faith, of course, are the living God, our Father, and his Son, the Lord Jesus Christ. We worship God in the name of his Only Begotten Son, through the power of the Holy Ghost. The appearance of these two heavenly Beings to the Prophet Joseph Smith in 1820 elevates him to that select center from which the very pulse of life for this Church has emanated. He was tutored by Deity and by their appointed angelic messengers. We are privileged to share those revealed truths as we study the holy scriptures. This theophany, transcendent in importance, with its heart-throbbing vitality, ushered in the work of the Restoration—the "restitution of all things" (see Acts 3:21) that had been promised centuries before.

Yet, as the work of the Restoration progresses, we can expect accelerating attacks from opposing forces. The enemy opposed the Church when first established in the early 1800s, and assaults from the enemy continue even today against the institutional Church and its members. Some of these attacks will be aimed at their peripheral activities, but the sharply focused thrusts of the future will chiefly be aimed at the heart of the Church—the prophetic mission of Joseph Smith and the doctrines he taught. The crucial fact of the matter is that Joseph Smith's integral role is central to this work. God knows it. We know it. Satan knows it, and so do many of those who follow satanic ideologies.

So, with the hope of assisting in your preparation for the attacks that will be directed at the heart of the Church, I will quote the Prophet, scriptures ancient and modern, and authoritative testimonies of eyewitnesses and of those who succeeded Joseph Smith as President of the Church.

Attacks have been authored by many, and more will yet write, to rationalize in mundane terms the work of Joseph Smith, the modern prophet. Indeed, his experiences may not be comprehended by a finite mind unaided by the Holy Spirit. Such was the case with Josiah Quincy, who rejected what he called the "monstrous claims" of Mormonism, but recognized Joseph Smith to be an extraordinary leader of unquestionable influence and power. In the closing paragraph of his essay on the Prophet, Quincy summed up his dilemma in these words:

> I have endeavored to give details of my visit to the Mormon Prophet with absolute accuracy. If the reader does not know just what to make of Joseph Smith, I

cannot help him out of the difficulty. I myself stand helpless before the puzzle.[1]

Some critics will arise from clusters of the so-called scholars or philosophers, or others schooled in scientific theory. Even the unschooled and the godless may take their turn stabbing barbs at the Prophet Joseph Smith.

But before one can accept a man as a prophet of God, one must first accept God. We declare that God lives and that he has frequently in times past spoken through his prophets so that they in turn may teach and testify to all of God's children upon the earth. Even though the worldly have repeatedly rejected prophets, that does not diminish the truths they have taught or the prophetic nature of their work.

In the high and holy calling to which I have been summoned, just as it is my conviction as a special witness to proclaim the divinity of Jesus Christ as our Lord and Savior, so it is my solemn privilege to proclaim the role of Joseph Smith as a prophet, seer, and revelator to this modern era, the dispensation of the fulness of times.

Joseph's own words provide eloquent evidence of this truth:

> I had actually seen a light, and in the midst of that light I saw two Personages, and they did in reality speak to me; and though I was hated and persecuted for saying that I had seen a vision, yet it was true; and while they were persecuting me, reviling me, and speaking all manner of evil against me falsely for so saying, I was led to say in my heart: Why persecute me for telling the truth? I have actually seen a vision; and who am I that I can withstand God, or why does the world think to make me deny what I have actually seen? For I had seen a vision; I knew it, and I knew that God knew it, and I could not deny it, neither dared I do

it; at least I knew that by so doing I would offend God, and come under condemnation. (JS–H 1:25)

The most prominent account of the First Vision, from which I have quoted, was prepared by the Prophet for publication in 1838. At least three other accounts of the vision were also recorded. These accounts were given under different circumstances to different audiences and for different purposes. Because each account emphasizes a different aspect of the same experience, some of the detractors of the Church have attempted to point out discrepancies in the several accounts. In the January 1985 *Ensign* appears a most noteworthy article by Milton V. Backman, Jr., entitled "Joseph Smith's Recitals of the First Vision." You will want to study this and become familiar with each of the recorded accounts of the First Vision so that you will not be disarmed if you hear that more than one account was given.

The 1838 account of the visitation of the Father and the Son is recorded in the Pearl of Great Price. It was approved by the Church as scripture. This means that it is the "will of the Lord, . . . the mind of the Lord, [and] . . . the word of the Lord" to the Saints (see D&C 68:4). No one can be a member of the Church in full faith who does not accept this testimony of Joseph Smith as truth.

In his account, Joseph Smith bore witness of the fact that he saw God the Father and his Son, Jesus Christ. It was more than a vision or a dream. These two heavenly, holy Personages appeared to him. The reality of that appearance is just as central to our theology as our declaration and belief in the atonement and resurrection of our Lord and Savior, Jesus the Christ. This theophany is at the very heart of our faith.

But this is not all. The bringing forth of the Book of Mormon and the restitution of the priesthood, which are also central to our faith, are realities occasioned through the further work of the Prophet Joseph Smith.

The Book of Mormon is a physical, tangible evidence of his prophetic calling. He declared the Book of Mormon to be a record of former inhabitants of ancient America who kept a record on golden plates. These plates, he said, were given to him by an angel of the Lord who came to him on an annual visitation on the same day of the same month over a period of four years. Finally the records were delivered into Joseph's hands for translation and subsequent publication. Today this record is known to the world as the Book of Mormon—Another Testament of Jesus Christ.

Opponents have tried to explain the origin of the Book of Mormon. Their explanations range from the discredited Solomon Spaulding manuscript theory to the idea that Sidney Rigdon collaborated with Joseph Smith in producing the manuscript. Some opponents even deny the account that an angel—a heavenly messenger—gave Joseph Smith custody of ancient records.

In fact, *many* heavenly messengers participated in the restoration of the Church. An eyewitness account to some of the impact of these revelations is shared with us by Joseph's mother, Lucy Mack Smith, who related the following recollection of evening conversations that took place in the Smith home after the visits of the angel Moroni to the Prophet:

> From this time forth [following Moroni's first visits in 1823], Joseph continued to receive instructions from the Lord, and we continued to get the children together every evening for the purpose of listening while he gave us a relation of the same. I presume our family

presented an aspect as singular as any that ever lived upon the face of the earth—all seated in a circle, father, mother, sons and daughters, and giving the most profound attention to a boy, eighteen years of age, who had never read the Bible through in his life: he seemed much less inclined to the perusal of books than any of the rest of our children, but far more given to meditation and deep study. . . .

During our evening conversations, Joseph would occasionally give us some of the most amusing recitals. . . . He would describe the ancient inhabitants of this continent, their dress, mode of traveling, and the animals upon which they rode; their cities, their buildings, with every particular; their mode of warfare; and also their religious worship. This he would do with as much ease, seemingly, *as if he had spent his whole life among them.*[2]

Where do you suppose Joseph got that information to describe the Nephite culture? How does one account for the fact that he could describe their culture as if he had spent his whole life among them? The answer: God revealed that information to him. He was God's appointed seer, and since truth includes knowledge of things as they were, God condescended to show him the civilizations of the Book of Mormon in order that Joseph might be prepared for his divine commission as a prophet on this consecrated land.

Another eyewitness account was given by John Taylor, a contemporary of Joseph Smith who later became third President of the Church:

Joseph Smith in the first place was set apart by the Almighty according to the counsels of the gods in the eternal worlds, to introduce the principles of life among the people, of which the Gospel is the grand power and influence, and through which salvation can extend to all peoples, all nations, all kindreds, all tongues and all worlds. It is the principle that brings life and immortality to light, and places us in communication with God. God selected him for that purpose, and he fulfilled his mission and lived honorably and died honorably. I know of what I speak for I was very well acquainted with him and was with him a great deal during his life, and was with him when he died. *The principles which he had, placed him in communication with the Lord, and not only with the Lord, but with the ancient apostles and prophets; such men, for instance, as Abraham, Isaac, Jacob, Noah, Adam, Seth, Enoch, and Jesus and the Father, and the apostles that lived on this continent as well as those who lived on the Asiatic continent. He seemed to be as familiar with these people as we are with one another.*[3]

Not only was the Prophet Joseph familiar with the culture of ancient civilizations, but I would again emphasize the words of John Taylor that he was "as familiar with [ancient prophets] as we are with one another." That tutoring process with heavenly beings and the spiritual giants of the past, I believe, was a marvelous preparation for the work the Lord had appointed for him to do.

Joseph knew of the doctrines imparted by Deity to Abraham and to Moses. Their sacred writings have become available to us by virtue of that inspired intimacy (see Moses and Abraham).

Another quiet clue to interchange with prophets of old is revealed in section seven of the Doctrine and Covenants. The explanatory heading of that section states that "the revelation is a translated version of the record made on parchment by John and hidden up by himself." This section contains a dialogue between the

Lord Jesus and John, the beloved disciple. John wrote while banished to the Isle of Patmos, one of the Greek islands. I marvel at the process by which information known to a prophet of one age and of one hemisphere is made known to another prophet of another hemisphere in another age. This transfer of knowledge seems to defy the ordinary mortal constraints of time and space.

Isn't it interesting that just as Joseph Smith knew of the writings of Abraham, Moses, John, and others, so did ancient prophets likewise know of Joseph Smith even millennia before he was born?

The eleventh son of Jacob, or Israel, was named Joseph. This patriarchal prophet saw that a choice seer named Joseph would come from his lineage. Hear these words of Lehi:

> Wherefore, Joseph truly saw our day. And he obtained a promise of the Lord, that out of the fruit of his loins the Lord God would raise up a righteous branch unto the house of Israel. . . .
>
> For Joseph truly testified, saying: A seer shall the Lord my God raise up, who shall be a choice seer unto the fruit of my loins.
>
> Yea, Joseph truly said: Thus saith the Lord unto me: A choice seer will I raise up out of the fruit of thy loins; and he shall be esteemed highly. . . . And unto him will I give commandment that he shall do a work for the fruit of thy loins, his brethren, which shall be of great worth unto them, even to the bringing of them to the knowledge of the covenants which I have made with thy fathers.
>
> And I will give unto him a commandment that he shall do none other work, save the work which I shall command him. And I will make him great in mine eyes for he shall do my work.

> And he shall be great like unto Moses, whom I have
> said I would raise up unto you, to deliver my people, O
> house of Israel. (2 Nephi 3:5–9)

You will note in this remarkable prophecy by Lehi to
his own son, whose name was also Joseph, that a latter-
day seer would be raised up from the lineage of Joseph,
son of Jacob, to bring Israel to a knowledge of their
covenants. But again review this sentence: "He shall do
none other work, save the work which I shall command
him. And I will make him great in mine eyes; for he shall
do my work" (2 Nephi 3:8).

Some critics have suggested that Joseph Smith failed
in his efforts to bring about the utopian society he con-
ceived. They say his economic program—the United
Order—failed, that Zion was not redeemed as he had
hoped, and that he finally went to his own martyrdom
because of a failure to obey the voice of the Spirit to him.
Other opponents continue to search for faults or short-
comings in the earthly activities of the Prophet. These
critics may be unmindful of two revelations that state
very clearly what Joseph was to accomplish and also the
limitations on the work the Lord gave him to do.

Shortly after the Lord revealed that Independence,
Missouri, was to be the "center place" of Zion (see D&C
57:2–3), a revelation was given 1 August 1831, the first
Sabbath day after the Prophet arrived in Jackson County,
Missouri. In this revelation the Lord told Joseph Smith
what he was to do:

> Behold, verily I say unto you, for this cause I have
> sent you—that you might be obedient, and that your
> hearts might be prepared to bear testimony of the
> things which are to come;
> And also that *you might be honored in laying the
> foundation,* and in bearing record of the land upon

which the Zion of God shall stand. (D&C 58:6–7; emphasis added)

A second revelation asserts that "the Prophet Joseph Smith, . . . Hyrum Smith, Brigham Young, John Taylor, Wilford Woodruff, and other choice spirits . . . were reserved to come forth in the fulness of times to take part in *laying the foundations* of the great latter-day work" (D&C 138:53; emphasis added).

In both these revelations, you will note the consistent limitation that was placed on the work the Lord gave to the Prophet Joseph. He and his early successors were only to "lay the foundation" of the great latter-day work. He was not to lead the Church into the millennial reign of the Lord, as some supposed. He was not to perfect the United Order. He did only that which the Lord told him to do—no more, no less. It would be left to others to build on the foundation which Joseph laid. In fact, the Lord revealed to Joseph Smith that certain conditions must be met before Zion was fully established: The Saints were first to be taught more perfectly, to gain experience and learn more about their duties, to become very great in numbers, and to become sanctified before the Lord (see D&C 105:10, 31).

Even now we can see that the amount of work that must yet be done portends that it will be some time before the Lord shall begin his millennial reign on earth. Meanwhile, as we patiently work toward that day, we reflect again on the fruits resulting from the foundations laid by the Prophet Joseph.

Jesus declared, "Ye shall know [prophets] by their fruits. . . . Every good tree bringeth forth good fruit" (Matthew 7:16–17). What are some of the fruits of Joseph's prophetic ministry?

The dynamic growth of the Church is certainly one of them. In October of 1831, while the Church was yet in its infancy, while there were no stakes or missions and the Church had less than a thousand members, the Prophet Joseph Smith offered a prayer by revelation, one verse from which I quote:

> The keys of the kingdom of God are committed unto man on the earth, and from thence shall the gospel roll forth unto the ends of the earth, as the stone which is cut out of the mountain without hands shall roll forth, until it has filled the whole earth. (D&C 65:2)

Using the imagery of the ancient prophet Daniel, this young man foretold that this little church would roll forth until it filled the whole earth.

One of the major challenges confronting the Church today is that imposed by its own phenomenal rate of growth. No wonder a prophecy made by the angel Moroni takes on such relevance today. This pronouncement was made when Joseph Smith was but seventeen years of age:

> [The angel Moroni] called me by name, and said unto me that he was a messenger sent from the presence of God to me . . . ; that God had a work for me to do; and that my name should be had for good and evil among all nations, kindreds, and tongues, or that it should be both good and evil spoken of among all people. (JS–H 1:33)

This was also foreseen in a special blessing given to the Prophet by the Patriarch Joseph Smith, Sr., in 1835:

> Thy testimony shall yet convince thousands and tens of thousands; it shall shine like the sun, and

though the wicked seek to overthrow it, it shall be in vain, for the Lord God shall bear it off victorious.[4]

Today the name of Joseph Smith is known far and wide. Either men praise him or revile him, but few remain neutral. Even the Prophet himself prepared us for the attacks that now come and will continue to be levied upon him. These are his words:

> I never told you I was perfect; but there is no error in the revelations which I have taught. Must I, then, be thrown away as a thing of naught?[5]

President George Albert Smith had this to say about those who would defame the Prophet:

> There have been some who have belittled him, but I would like to say that those who have done so will be forgotten and their remains will go back to mother earth, if they have not already gone, and the odor of their infamy will never die, while the glory and honor and majesty and courage and fidelity manifested by the Prophet Joseph Smith will attach to his name forever.[6]

These warnings notwithstanding, there will still be those who grovel for a word or a thought that would cast in poor light the Prophet Joseph Smith and his work. But the wise know that a single word or a single communication must not be viewed nor contorted beyond the importance of all else an individual may have said or done.

Even at the time of Jesus, people searched for a particular word to confuse his ministry. Those who conspired against Jesus deliberately sought "to provoke him to speak of many things . . . to catch something out of his mouth, that they might accuse him" (Luke 11:53–54). Those conspiring against Jesus, particularly the

Pharisees, actually "took counsel how they might entangle him in his talk" (Matthew 22:15).

Paul, testifying before Agrippa and the Jewish hierarchy, indicated that he had been called by the Lord to go to the *gentiles*. At once, the word *gentiles* offended the audience: "Away with such a fellow from the earth: for it is not fit that he should live. And . . . they . . . cast off their clothes, and threw dust into the air" (Acts 22:21–23). Paul was made an offender for a single word!

Isaiah, who foretold many details of the Book of Mormon and the attacks that would come upon the prophet responsible for its translation, saw that Paul's fate would beset Joseph. Isaiah wrote:

> [Those] that watch for iniquity . . . [would] make a man an offender for a word, and lay a snare for him that reproveth in the gate, and turn aside the just for a thing of nought. (Isaiah 29:20–21)

Prophets ancient and modern have risen above the obstacles imposed by offenders and have addressed themselves to the mighty missionary endeavors assigned to them by their Lord and Master.

The Prophet Joseph Smith made two statements on separate occasions that, to some critics, may seem contradictory. He said, "The greatest and most important duty is to preach the Gospel."[7] He also said, "The greatest responsibility in this world that God has laid upon us is to seek after our dead."[8] These statements, in fact, are not contradictory since both involve the saving of souls. The first statement focuses on saving the souls of the living; the second, on saving the souls of the dead.

The importance of salvation for both the living and the dead as a prelude to the Millennium was declared by Jesus:

> And this gospel of the kingdom shall be preached in
> all the world for a witness unto all nations; and then
> shall the end come. (Matthew 24:14)

But the missionary work among the five billion inhabitants of the earth is dwarfed by the relative magnitude of the assignment to bring salvation to the many billions of deceased souls who never had the opportunity to hear the gospel while living. There is no doctrine that demonstrates the mercy and love of God, the Father, for his children more than the doctrine of salvation for the dead, while at the same time giving men and women today opportunities for Christlike service to others.

So many fruits of the bounteous labors of the Prophet Joseph Smith stand today as evidence of his prophetic ministry. The Church is restored with its priesthood authority. Ordinances have been revealed that bless lives here and hereafter. Doctrines of Deity are recorded in Joseph's translated and inspired writings, which are so monumental in scope that they nearly defy description.

Can anything exceed the conviction and sincerity of testimony as it was delivered by the man whose wife and children clung to him as he went like "a lamb to the slaughter"?

Yes, one of the most convincing evidences of the commitment of the Prophet to the truth for which he lived, and to the cause for which he died, was the resolute certitude of his statements as he approached his death. Here is one example as recorded by an eyewitness, Dan Jones. These, he reported, were the Prophet's words:

> I do not fear the consequence, be it even the most
> horrible death, as much as I fear dying with a blemish
> on my character, or for the world to disgrace the reli-
> gion which I profess.[9]

I add my voice to those leaders contemporary with the Prophet who paid this tribute to him:

> Joseph Smith, the Prophet and Seer of the Lord, has done more, save Jesus only, for the salvation of men in this world, than any other man that ever lived in it. In the short space of twenty years, he has brought forth the Book of Mormon, which he translated by the gift and power of God, and has been the means of publishing it on two continents; has sent the fulness of the everlasting gospel, which it contained, to the four quarters of the earth; has brought forth the revelations and commandments which compose this book of Doctrine and Covenants, and many other wise documents and instructions for the benefit of the children of men; gathered many thousands of the Latter-day Saints, founded a great city, and left a fame and name that cannot be slain. He lived great, and he died great in the eyes of God and his people; and like most of the Lord's anointed in ancient times, has sealed his mission and his works with his own blood. (D&C 135:3)

To be as authoritative as possible, I have quoted scripture and competent authority, even prophetic and presidential. But there is another witness. I, too, have fasted and prayed, studied and searched to know for myself the truth of these things.

During decades prior to my call to the Twelve, I, with Sister Nelson, have been to the place of the Prophet's birth in Vermont and to the vicinity of his childhood, where he was operated upon without the mercy of an anesthetic. I have trod their farmland in the State of New York and have reverently entered that grove made sacred by his First Vision in 1820. I have climbed Cumorah's Hill as well as the steps of Kirtland's Temple inwardly rejoicing in the experiences he had there. I have wept for him at the jails of Liberty and Carthage. Now, I do know for myself that these things are true. The Lord God has manifest them unto me by the power of his Spirit. This is the witness of revelation which is in me.

I testify not only to the reality that God lives, that Jesus is the Christ, that this is his church restored in these latter days, but I fervently and sincerely declare that Joseph Smith is a prophet of God foreordained from before the foundations of the earth to the mission assigned to him, for which he paid with his life. I commit myself to continue the work, building on the foundation that he laid, in full recognition that each of the Lord's anointed risks his all for that commitment as did the Prophet Joseph Smith.

NOTES

1. *Figures of the Past* (Boston, 1883), p. 400.
2. Lucy Mack Smith, *History of Joseph Smith*, ed. Preston Nibley (Salt Lake City, 1979), pp. 82–83; emphasis added.
3. In *Journal of Discourses*, 21:94; emphasis added.
4. Quoted in *Church News*, 9 Sept. 1984, p. 6.
5. *Teachings of the Prophet Joseph Smith*, sel. Joseph Fielding Smith (Salt Lake City: Deseret Book Co., 1938), p. 368.
6. In Conference Report, Apr. 1948, pp. 181–82.
7. *Teachings of the Prophet Joseph Smith*, p. 113.
8. Ibid., p. 356.
9. Dan Jones, "The Martyrdom of Joseph Smith and His Brother, Hyrum!" *BYU Studies* 24 (Winter 1984): 86.

chapter 7

APOSTASY AND RESTORATION

ELDER DALLIN H. OAKS

The Church of Jesus Christ of Latter-day Saints has many beliefs in common with other Christian churches. But we have differences, and those differences explain why we send missionaries to other Christians, why we build temples in addition to churches, and why our beliefs bring us such happiness and strength to deal with the challenges of life and death. I wish to discuss some of the important additions our doctrines make to the Christian faith. My subject is apostasy and restoration.

In 1994, searchers discovered a Roman fort and city in the Sinai close to the Suez Canal. Though once a major city, its location had been covered by desert sands and its existence had been forgotten for hundreds of years.[1] Discoveries like this contradict the common assumption that knowledge increases with the passage of time. In fact, on some matters the general knowledge of mankind regresses as some important truths are distorted or ignored and eventually forgotten. For example, the American Indians were in many respects more successful at living in harmony with nature than our modern society. Similarly, modern artists and craftsmen have been unable to recapture some of the superior techniques and materials of the past, like the varnish on a Stradivarius violin.

We would be wiser if we could restore the knowledge of some important things that have been distorted, ignored, or forgotten. This also applies to religious knowledge. It explains the need for the gospel restoration we proclaim.

When Joseph Smith was asked to explain the major tenets of our faith, he wrote what we now call the Articles of Faith. The first article states, "We believe in God, the Eternal Father, and in His Son, Jesus Christ, and in the Holy Ghost." The Prophet later declared that "the simple and first principles of the gospel" include knowing "for a certainty the character of God."[2] We must begin with the truth about God and our relationship to him. Everything else follows from that.

In common with the rest of Christianity, we believe in a Godhead of Father, Son, and Holy Ghost. However, we testify that these three members of the Godhead are three separate and distinct beings. We also testify that God the Father is not just a spirit but is a glorified person with a tangible body, as is his resurrected Son, Jesus Christ.

When first communicated to mankind by prophets, the teachings we now have in the Bible were "plain and pure, and most precious and easy" to understand (1 Nephi 14:23). Even in the transmitted and translated version we have today, the Bible language confirms that God the Father and his resurrected Son, Jesus Christ, are tangible, separate beings. To cite only two of many such teachings, the Bible declares that man was created in the image of God, and it describes three separate members of the Godhead manifested at the baptism of Jesus (see Genesis 1:27; Matthew 3:13–17).

In contrast, many Christians reject the idea of a tangible, personal God and a Godhead of three separate beings. They believe that God is a spirit and that the Godhead is only one God. In our view, these concepts are evidence of the falling away we call the Great Apostasy.

We maintain that the concepts identified by such nonscriptural terms as "the incomprehensible mystery of God" and "the mystery of the Holy Trinity" are attributable to the ideas of Greek philosophy. These philosophical concepts transformed Christianity in the first few centuries following the deaths of the Apostles. For example, philosophers then maintained that physical matter was evil and that God was a spirit without feelings or passions. Persons of this persuasion, including learned men who became influential converts to Christianity, had a hard time accepting the simple teachings of early Christianity: an Only Begotten Son who said he was in the express image of his Father in Heaven and who taught his followers to be one as he and his Father were one, and a Messiah who died on a cross and later appeared to his followers as a resurrected being with flesh and bones.

The collision between the speculative world of Greek philosophy and the simple, literal faith and practice of the earliest Christians produced sharp contentions that threatened to widen political divisions in the fragmenting Roman empire. This led Emperor Constantine to convene the first churchwide council in A.D. 325. The action of this council of Nicea remains the most important single event after the death of the Apostles in formulating the modern Christian concept of deity. The Nicean Creed erased the idea of the separate being of Father and Son by defining God the Son as being of "one substance with the Father."

Other councils followed, and from their decisions and the writings of churchmen and philosophers there came a synthesis of Greek philosophy and Christian doctrine in which the orthodox Christians of that day lost the fulness of truth about the nature of God and the Godhead. The consequences persist in the various creeds of Christianity, which declare a Godhead of only one being and which describe that single being or God as "incomprehensible" and "without body, parts, or passions." One of the distinguishing features of the doctrine of The Church of Jesus Christ of Latter-day Saints is its rejection of all of these postbiblical creeds.[3]

In the process of what we call the Apostasy, the tangible, personal God described in the Old and New Testaments was replaced by the abstract, incomprehensible deity defined by compromise with the speculative principles of Greek philosophy. The received language of the Bible remained, but the so-called "hidden meanings" of scriptural words were now explained in the vocabulary of a philosophy alien to their origins. In the language of that philosophy, God the Father ceased to be a Father in any but an allegorical sense. He ceased to exist as a comprehensible and compassionate being. And the separate identity of his Only Begotten Son was swallowed up in a philosophical abstraction that attempted to define a common substance and an incomprehensible relationship.

These descriptions of a religious philosophy are surely undiplomatic, but I hasten to add that Latter-day Saints do not apply such criticism to the men and women who profess these beliefs. We believe that most religious leaders and followers are sincere believers who love God and understand and serve him to the best of their abilities. We are indebted to the men and women who kept the light of faith and learning alive through the centuries to the present day. We have only to contrast the lesser light that exists among peoples unfamiliar with the names of God and Jesus Christ to realize the great contribution made by Christian teachers through the ages. We honor them as servants of God.

Then came the First Vision. An unschooled boy, seeking knowledge from the ultimate source, saw two personages of indescribable brightness and glory and heard one of them say, while pointing to the other, "This is My Beloved Son. Hear Him!" (JS–H 1:17). The divine teaching in that vision began the restoration of the fulness of the gospel of Jesus Christ. God the Son told the boy prophet that all the "creeds" of the churches of that day "were an abomination in his sight" (v. 19). We affirm that this divine declaration was a condemnation of the creeds, not of the faithful seekers who believed in them. Joseph Smith's First Vision showed that the prevailing concepts of the nature of God and the Godhead were untrue and could not lead their adherents to the destiny God desired for them.

After a subsequent outpouring of modern scripture and revelation, this modern prophet declared, "The Father has a body of flesh and bones as tangible as man's; the Son also; but the Holy Ghost has not a body of flesh and bones, but is a personage of Spirit" (D&C 130:22).

This belief does not mean that we claim sufficient spiritual maturity to comprehend God. Nor do we equate our imperfect mortal bodies to his immortal, glorified being. But we can comprehend the fundamentals he has revealed about himself and the other members of the

Godhead. And that knowledge is essential to our understanding of the purpose of mortal life and of our eternal destiny as resurrected beings after mortal life.

In the theology of the restored church of Jesus Christ, the purpose of mortal life is to prepare us to realize our destiny as sons and daughters of God—to become like Him. Joseph Smith and Brigham Young both taught that "no man . . . can know himself unless he knows God, and he can not know God unless he knows himself."[4] The Bible describes mortals as "the children of God" and as "heirs of God, and joint-heirs with Christ" (Romans 8:16–17). It also declares that "we suffer with him, that we may be also glorified together" (Romans 8:17) and that "when he shall appear, we shall be like him" (1 John 3:2). We take these Bible teachings literally. We believe that the purpose of mortal life is to acquire a physical body and, through the atonement of Jesus Christ and by obedience to the laws and ordinances of the gospel, to qualify for the glorified, resurrected celestial state that is called exaltation or eternal life.

Like other Christians, we believe in a heaven or paradise and a hell following mortal life, but to us that two-part division of the righteous and the wicked is merely temporary, while the spirits of the dead await their resurrections and final judgments. The destinations that follow the final judgments are much more diverse. Our restored knowledge of the separateness of the three members of the Godhead provides a key to help us understand the diversities of resurrected glory.

In their final judgment, the children of God will be assigned to a kingdom of glory for which their obedience has qualified them. In his letters to the Corinthians, the Apostle Paul described these places. He told of a vision in which he was "caught up to the third heaven" and "heard unspeakable words, which it is not lawful for a man to utter" (2 Corinthians 12:2, 4). Speaking of the resurrection of the dead, he described "celestial bodies," "bodies terrestrial" (1 Corinthians 15:40), and "bodies telestial" (JST, 1 Corinthians 15:40), each pertaining to a different degree of glory. He likened these different glories to the sun, to the moon, and to different stars (see 1 Corinthians 15:41).

We learn from modern revelation that these three different degrees of glory have a special relationship to the three different members of the Godhead.

The lowest degree is the telestial domain of those who "received not the gospel, neither the testimony of Jesus, neither the prophets" (D&C 76:101) and who have had to suffer for their wickedness. But even this degree has a glory that "surpasses all understanding" (D&C 76:89). Its occupants receive the Holy Spirit and the administering of angels, for even those who have been wicked will ultimately be "heirs of [this degree of] salvation" (D&C 76:88).

The next higher degree of glory, the terrestrial, "excels in all things the glory of the telestial, even in glory, and in power, and in might, and in dominion" (D&C 76:91). The terrestrial is the abode of those who were the "honorable men of the earth" (D&C 76:75). Its most distinguishing feature is that those who qualify for terrestrial glory "receive of the presence of the Son" (v. 77). Concepts familiar to all Christians might liken this higher kingdom to heaven because it has the presence of the Son.

In contrast to traditional Christianity, we join with Paul in affirming the existence of a third or higher heaven. Modern revelation describes it as the celestial kingdom—the abode of those "whose bodies are celestial, whose glory is that of the sun, even the glory of God" (D&C 76:70). Those who qualify for this kingdom of glory "shall dwell in the presence of God and his Christ forever and ever" (D&C 76:62). Those who have met the highest requirements for this kingdom, including faithfulness to covenants made in a temple of God and marriage for eternity, will be exalted to the godlike state referred to as the "fulness" of the Father or eternal life (see D&C 76:56, 94; see also D&C 131; 132:19–20). (This destiny of eternal life or God's life should be familiar to all who have studied the ancient Christian doctrine of and belief in deification or apotheosis.) For us, eternal life is not a mystical union with an incomprehensible spirit-god. Eternal life is family life with a loving Father in Heaven and with our progenitors and our posterity.

The theology of the restored gospel of Jesus Christ is comprehensive, universal, merciful, and true. Following the necessary experience of mortal life, all sons and daughters of God will ultimately be resurrected and go to a kingdom of glory. The righteous—regardless of current religious denomination or belief—will ultimately go to a kingdom of glory more wonderful than any of us can comprehend. Even the wicked, or almost all of them, will ultimately go to a marvelous—though lesser—kingdom of glory. All of that will occur because of God's love for his children and because of the atonement and resurrection of Jesus Christ, "who glorifies the Father, and saves all the works of his hands" (D&C 76:43).

The purpose of The Church of Jesus Christ of Latter-day Saints is to help all of the children of God understand their potential and achieve their highest destiny. This church exists to provide the sons and daughters of God with the means of entrance into and exaltation in the celestial kingdom. This is a family-centered church in doctrine and practices. Our understanding of the nature and purpose of God the Eternal Father explains our destiny and our relationship in his eternal family. Our theology begins with heavenly parents. Our highest aspiration is to be like them. Under the merciful plan of the Father, all of this is possible through the atonement of the Only Begotten of the Father, our Lord and Savior, Jesus Christ. As earthly parents we participate in the gospel plan by providing mortal bodies for the spirit children of God. The fulness of eternal salvation is a family matter.

It is the reality of these glorious possibilities that causes us to proclaim our message of restored Christianity to all people, even to good practicing Christians with other beliefs. This is why we build temples. This is the faith that gives us strength and joy to confront the challenges of mortal life. We offer these truths and opportunities to all people and testify to their truthfulness.

NOTES

1. See "Remains of Roman Fortress Emerge from Sinai Desert," *Deseret News*, 6 Oct. 1994, p. A20.
2. "Conference Minutes," *Times and Seasons*, 15 Aug. 1844, p. 614.
3. See Stephen E. Robinson, *Are Mormons Christians?* (Salt Lake City: Bookcraft, 1991); Daniel H. Ludlow, ed., *Encyclopedia of Mormonism*, 5 vols. (New York: Macmillan, 1992), s.v. "apostasy," "doctrine," "God the Father," and "Godhead."
4. In *Journal of Discourses*, 16:75; see also *The Words of Joseph Smith*, ed. Andrew F. Ehat and Lyndon W. Cook (Provo, Utah: Religious Studies Center, Brigham Young University, 1980), p. 340.

CHAPTER 8

HYRUM SMITH: "FIRM AS THE PILLARS OF HEAVEN"

ELDER M. RUSSELL BALLARD

During the early part of July 1995, Sister Ballard and I had the opportunity to travel to Church historic sites in Palmyra, Kirtland, and Nauvoo with our seven children, their companions, and twenty of our grandchildren. Our tour of these locations filled our souls with an ever greater love and respect for the Prophet Joseph Smith, for his family, and for the stalwarts who first embraced the restored gospel of Jesus Christ and became members of The Church of Jesus Christ of Latter-day Saints. What an extraordinary experience it was to teach my family from the Doctrine and Covenants while standing on the very ground where many of those revelations and instructions were received.

Visiting those inspirational sites and immersing ourselves as a family into the events of the Restoration reminded me again of the marvelous privilege we have to live in a day when we have such clear doctrinal understanding of our Heavenly Father's plan for the salvation and exaltation of his children. The clarity of our relationship to the Lord Jesus Christ and his restored church is precious, empowering knowledge for each one of us. I thank God that in these difficult days of moral decay and departure from sound values, we have no shortage of revealed truth to guide our lives.

The Spirit has confirmed to me the important responsibility we have to see that the legacy of faith of our pioneer forefathers is never lost. We can derive great strength, particularly our youth, from understanding our church history. As a descendant of Hyrum Smith, I feel a solemn obligation to ensure that the Church never forgets the significant ministry of this great leader. Recognizing that no one save Jesus only excels the singular accomplishment of the Prophet Joseph, I am stirred within my soul to remember and respect the valiant life and remarkable contributions of his older brother, the patriarch Hyrum.

In September of 1840, Joseph Smith, Sr., gathered his family around him. This venerable patriarch was dying and wanted to leave his blessing on his beloved wife and children. Hyrum, the eldest living son, asked his father to intercede with heaven when he arrived there so the enemies of the Church "may not have so much power" over the Latter-day Saints. Father Smith then laid his hands upon Hyrum's head and blessed him to have "peace . . . sufficient . . . to accomplish the work which God has given you to do." Knowing of Hyrum's lifelong faithfulness, he concluded this last blessing with the promise that Hyrum would "be as firm as the pillars of heaven unto the end of [his] days."[1]

This blessing identified Hyrum's strongest characteristic. More than anything else, he was "firm as the pillars of heaven." Throughout Hyrum's life, the forces of evil combined against him in an attempt to defeat him or at least to prompt him to stray off course.

After his older brother Alvin's death in 1823, Hyrum bore significant responsibility in the Smith family. At the same time, he assisted and served his brother, Joseph the Prophet, throughout the long and arduous process of the Restoration. Ultimately, he joined Joseph and other martyrs of past gospel dispensations. His blood was shed as his final testimony to the world.

Through it all, Hyrum stood firm. He knew the course his life would take, and he consciously chose to follow it. To Joseph, Hyrum became companion, protector, provider, confidant, and eventually joined him as a martyr. Unjust persecution engulfed them throughout their lives. Although he was older, Hyrum recognized his brother's divine mantle. While he gave Joseph strong counsel on occasion, Hyrum always deferred to his younger brother.

Speaking to his brother, Joseph once said, "Brother Hyrum, what a faithful heart you have got! Oh may the Eternal Jehovah crown eternal blessings upon your head, as a reward for the care you have had for my soul! O how many are the sorrows we have shared together."[2]

On another occasion, Joseph referred to his brother with these profound and tender words: "I love him with that love that is stronger than death."[3]

Hyrum gave unfailing service to the Church. In 1829 he was among a handful of individuals who were allowed to view the gold plates from which the Book of Mormon was translated, and for the rest of his life he testified to the divine nature of the Book of Mormon as one of the Eight Witnesses who "had seen the plates with his eyes and handled them with his hands."[4] He was among the first to be baptized in this gospel dispensation. At age thirty, he was the oldest of the six men chosen in 1830 to formally organize The Church of Jesus Christ of Latter-day Saints. In 1831, he stood before the Ohio conference and pledged "that all he had was the Lord's and he was ready to do his will continually."[5] In 1833, when the Lord chastised the Church for delaying the start of the Kirtland Temple, Hyrum was the first to start digging its foundation. As a member of the temple committee, Hyrum rallied the Church to perform the seemingly impossible task of building the Kirtland Temple when most Church members literally had nothing to give to the cause. A few years later he repeated this service with the building of the Nauvoo Temple.

Hyrum served in the Ohio bishopric, on the first high council, as Patriarch, as a counselor in the First Presidency, and finally as one of only two men ever to hold the office of Assistant President of the Church.

Hyrum served many missions for the Church. During one mission, traveling from Kirtland to Missouri, he endured one of his greatest trials when his first wife, Jerusha, died soon after giving birth to his sixth child. Hyrum's mother, Lucy Mack Smith, wrote that Jerusha's death "wrung our hearts with more than common grief. . . . She was a woman whom everybody loved."[6]

Although Hyrum was grieved, his faith was unshaken; his determination to serve Heavenly Father and his church never faltered. I believe God rewarded his faithfulness by bringing into his life one of the great women of Church history, Mary Fielding, whom he subsequently married. Together they built an extraordinary legacy of love and discipleship.

Clearly, Hyrum Smith was one of the firm pillars of the Restoration. But sadly, many Church members know little about him except that he was martyred with his brother in Carthage Jail. That is significant, but he did far more. Indeed, Joseph Smith himself once suggested that his followers would do well to pattern their lives after Hyrum's.[7] May I suggest a few examples from Hyrum's life that we may wish to follow.

In 1829, when Joseph was finishing the translation of the Book of Mormon, Hyrum was anxious to begin spreading the gospel and building the Church. He asked Joseph to inquire of the Lord what he should do. In section eleven of the Doctrine and Covenants we read the Lord's response: "Seek not to declare my word, but first seek to obtain my word. . . . Study my word which hath gone forth . . . , and also study my word . . . which is now translating" (vv. 21–22).

Hyrum's life is a witness to his obedience to this instruction. To the very last day of his life, he devoted himself to obtaining the word through study of the scriptures. In Carthage Jail, he read and commented on extracts from the Book of Mormon. The scriptures were obviously part of Hyrum's being, and he turned to them during times when he needed comfort and strength the most.

Just think of the spiritual strength we could gain in our lives and how much more effective we would be as teachers, missionaries, and friends if we studied the scriptures regularly. I am sure we, like Hyrum, will be able to endure our greatest trials if we search the word of God as he did.

The second great example from Hyrum's life that we may wish to follow occurred very early in the Restoration. According to Lucy Mack Smith, when young Joseph first told the rest of the family about his experience in the Sacred Grove, Hyrum and all the others received the message "joyfully." The family sat "in a circle, . . . giving the most profound attention to a boy . . . who had never read the Bible through in his life."[8] In contrast to the reaction of Laman and Lemuel to their younger brother Nephi's divine calling and to the jealousy of the older brothers of Joseph who was sold into Egypt, there was no jealousy or animosity in Hyrum Smith. Instead, real faith was born in him of the simple and joyful response he felt to the spiritual truth of his brother's message. The Lord let him know in his heart what was right, and he followed Joseph—faithfully—for the rest of his life.

"I, the Lord, love [Hyrum]," the Savior revealed in section 124 of the Doctrine and Covenants, "because of the integrity of his heart, and because he loveth that which is right before me" (v. 15).

Faithful Hyrum had a believing heart; he did not have to see everything Joseph saw. For him, hearing the truth from Joseph's lips and feeling the spiritual promptings whispering that it was true were enough. Faith to believe was the source of Hyrum's spiritual strength and is the source of the spiritual strength of faithful members of the Church then and today. We do not need more members who question every detail; we need members who have felt with their hearts, who live close to the Spirit, and who follow its promptings joyfully. We need seeking hearts and minds that welcome gospel truths without argument or complaint and without requiring miraculous manifestation. Oh, how we are blessed when members respond joyfully to counsel from their bishops, stake presidents, quorum or auxiliary leaders, some of whom might be younger than they and less experienced. What great blessings we receive when we follow "that which is right" joyfully and not grudgingly.

The third example from the life of Hyrum was his selfless service to others. His mother commented on this quality, saying that he was "rather remarkable for his tenderness and sympathy."[9] When Joseph was afflicted with severe pain in his leg, Hyrum relieved his mother and sat beside Joseph almost twenty-four hours a day for more than a week.

Hyrum was the first to extend a hand of friendship to a visitor, the first to attempt to moderate a dispute, the first to forgive an enemy. The Prophet Joseph was known to say that "if Hyrum could not make peace between two who had fallen out, the angels themselves might not hope to accomplish the task."[10]

Do similar needs exist in the Church and in our families today? Are we sensitive to the concerns of those who need special attention? Are we aware of families who are struggling spiritually or emotionally and who need our love, encouragement, and support? Hyrum's example of selfless service could be a powerful influence in the world today if enough of us chose to follow it.

Another great example comes to us from the dark dungeon of Liberty Jail. Here Hyrum, Joseph, and a few others suffered exposure to cold, hunger, inhumane treatment, and the loneliness of isolation from friends. In this schoolhouse jail, Hyrum learned the lesson of patience in adversity and affliction. In the midst of this most severe trial, his primary concern was not for himself and his companions but for his family. In a letter to his wife,

Hyrum wrote that the "greatest part of my trouble" was wondering how she and the family were doing. "When I think of your trouble my heart is weighed down with sorrow. . . . But what can I do? . . . Thy will be done O Lord."[11]

As I travel throughout the Church, I see members being tried in the crucible of affliction. I see members suffering from debilitating health concerns. I see husbands, wives, and parents living in trying circumstances they cannot change regarding their spouses or their children. Every one of us is faced at times with unpleasant situations, adversity, and affliction that we cannot change. Many circumstances can only be addressed with time, tears, prayer, and faith. For us, like Hyrum, peace may only come when we bring ourselves to say, "But what can I do? . . . Thy will be done O Lord."

Surely Joseph was inspired when he wrote of his brother Hyrum, "Thy name shall be written . . . for those who come after thee to look upon, that they may pattern after thy works."[12] May we help keep the promise made to Hyrum in section 124 of the Doctrine and Covenants that his "name [shall] be had in honorable remembrance from generation to generation, forever and ever" (v. 96). His name most certainly will be honorably revered as we follow his example and "pattern after [his] works." May the memory of Hyrum Smith and all of our faithful forefathers never fade from our minds.

NOTES

1. Lucy Mack Smith, *History of Joseph Smith*, ed. Preston Nibley (Salt Lake City: Bookcraft, 1979), p. 309.
2. *History of the Church*, 5:107–8.
3. Ibid., 2:338.
4. Letter of Sally Parker to Francis Tufts, 26 Aug. 1838; quoted in Richard Lloyd Anderson, *Investigating the Book of Mormon Witnesses* (Salt Lake City: Deseret Book Co., 1981), pp. 158–59.

5. Quoted in Donald Q. Cannon and Lyndon W. Cook, eds., *Far West Record: Minutes of The Church of Jesus Christ of Latter-day Saints, 1830–44* (Salt Lake City: Deseret Book Co., 1983), p. 21.
6. *History of Joseph Smith*, p. 246.
7. *History of the Church*, 5:108.
8. *History of Joseph Smith*, p. 82.
9. Ibid., p. 55.
10. Quoted in J. P. Widtsoe Osborne, "Hyrum Smith, Patriarch," *Utah Genealogical and Historical Magazine*, Apr. 1911, p. 56.
11. Letter of Hyrum Smith to Mary Fielding Smith, Liberty Jail, 16 March 1839, Mary Fielding Smith Collectoin, LDS Church Archives.
12. *History of the Church*, 5:108.

THE EXAMPLE OF JOSEPH SMITH

ELDER JOSEPH B. WIRTHLIN

A timid elder from a small town, new in the mission field, hears these words: "You don't really believe that Joseph Smith story yourself." Then the door abruptly closes and he walks down the path. Suddenly he stops, retraces his steps, and knocks at the door. Though he is frightened, he speaks loudly: "You said I didn't know Joseph Smith was a prophet of God. I want you to know that I know he is, and I know he translated the Book of Mormon. I know he saw God, the Father, and His Son, Jesus Christ."

Almost halfway around the world, another young man is confronted by one who has a superior education. The young man does not have the knowledge or the training to meet the other man's arguments. Suddenly he stands up, looks directly into the eyes of the man with the fine education, grips him by the shoulders, and says, "I haven't had much education. My father died when I was fourteen, and I have been running a ranch to help support my mother and brothers and sisters. But I know that Joseph Smith is a prophet of God."

What a lasting impact this latter-day prophet has had upon the lives of a large segment of mankind!

A great tribute to the Prophet, written by Elder John Taylor, a witness to the events of his martyrdom, is found in section 135 of the Doctrine and Covenants:

> Joseph Smith, the Prophet and Seer of the Lord, has done more, save Jesus only, for the salvation of men in this world, than any other man that ever lived in it. In the short space of twenty years, he has brought forth the Book of Mormon, which he translated by the gift and power of God, and has been the means of publishing it on two continents; has sent the fulness of the everlasting gospel, which it contained, to the four quarters of the earth; has brought forth the revelations and commandments which compose this book of Doctrine and Covenants, and many other wise documents and instructions for the benefit of the children of men; gathered many thousands of the Latter-day Saints, founded a great city, and left a fame and name that cannot be slain. He lived great, and he died great in the eyes of God and his people; and like most of the Lord's anointed in ancient times, has sealed his mission and his works with his own blood; and so has his brother Hyrum. In life they were not divided, and in death they were not separated! (D&C 135:3)

From this, we learn that Joseph Smith, a prophet of God, had the most important assignment on this earth with the exception of Jesus Christ.

Joseph Smith—a man untrained in theology—brought forth more printed pages of scripture than the combined pages from such scripture writers as Moses, Luke, and Paul. These include his translations of the Book of Mormon and the Pearl of Great Price, the revelations found in the Doctrine and Covenants, the writings in the Pearl of Great Price, and his revisions of portions of the Bible. What came through him was clearly beyond his natural abilities.

The Prophet's great achievements did not lie alone in prophesying, in speaking, or in writing, but also in what he was. One writer wrote: "A man's true greatness is not in what he says he is, nor in what people say he is; his greatness lies in what he really is. What he really is may be determined by how he acts in unguarded moments alone with his family or close friends."[1] As President John Taylor said of Joseph Smith, "He lived great."

John M. Bernhisel, a man known for his integrity, wrote:

> Having been a boarder in General Smith's family for more than nine months, and having therefore had abundant opportunities of contemplating his character and observing his conduct, I have concluded to give you a few of my "impressions" of him.
>
> General Joseph Smith is naturally a man of strong mental powers, and is possessed of much energy and decision of character, great penetration, and a profound knowledge of human nature. He is man of calm judgment, enlarged views, and is eminently distinguished by his love of justice. He is kind and obliging, generous and benevolent, sociable and cheerful, and is possessed of a mind of a contemplative and reflective character. He is honest, frank, fearless and independent. . . .
>
> But it is in the gentle charities of domestic life, as the tender and affectionate husband and parent, the warm and sympathizing friend, that the prominent traits of his character are revealed, and his heart is felt to be keenly alive to the kindest and softest emotions of which human nature is susceptible. . . .

. . . As a religious teacher, as well as a man, he is greatly beloved by this people.[2]

Wilford Woodruff made the following excellent and succinct observation: "I have felt to rejoice exceedingly of what I saw of brother Joseph, for in his public and private career he carried with him the Spirit of the Almighty, and he manifested a greatness of soul which I have never seen in any other man."[3]

Joseph Smith's greatness of soul drew many others to him. On one occasion, after delivering a sermon to a gathering of Saints, he was arrested by the sheriff, who was in league with a group of individuals who disliked the Prophet intensely. However, the sheriff was so impressed with the Prophet after being in his presence just a few minutes that he realized he had been deceived concerning the character of the man he had arrested. He had agreed to deliver Joseph into the hands of those enemies, but when he and his prisoner approached the mob, he whipped his horse and raced past them. Stunned, they gave chase but were soon left in the distance. They stopped at an inn for the night, and the sheriff gave the Prophet the bed while he himself lay on the floor with his feet against the door and his pistol in his hand. He was determined to assure the safety of this man whom, just a few hours before, he had considered a despicable individual.[4]

It is important to be a great prophet, but one cannot be a great prophet without being a great man, "for of the abundance of the heart his mouth speaketh" (Luke 6:45).

John A. Widtsoe, a member of the Council of the Twelve from 1921 to 1952, wrote: "Greatness is a product of many causes. It is like the mighty flowing river, fed and made possible by thousands of mountain rivulets. Even so with Joseph Smith. The reflection from innumerable facets of his character makes up the picture of Joseph Smith's greatness."[5]

Those who lived as contemporaries of Joseph Smith had the advantage of knowing him personally, but we who live a century and a half after his martyrdom are not without advantage. We have the advantage of perspective. Time has a way of supporting those who are truly great and exposing those who would feign greatness. The Lord called Joseph not just to be an example and guide to those of his own day but to benefit, through his teachings, those who would come after.

Elder Widtsoe noted that Joseph Smith had four qualities that made him great and were "the cornerstones of his character":

> (1) He had unchanging faith and trust in God. (2) He loved truth. (3) He was humble. (4) He loved his fellowmen. These qualities always lead to greatness. Without them there is no true greatness.
>
> Doubt did not belong to Joseph Smith's nature. The Prophet's faith in God—in His existence, reality, and relationship to man—was superb. Joseph took God at his word, as in the First Vision.[6]

Joseph Smith lacked knowledge, but through prayer he approached God in faith, and an answer was given to him (see James 1:5). Throughout his life he took counsel with the Almighty and did not try to act alone upon his own judgment. He accepted the responsibility of restoring the kingdom of God on earth. In spite of brutal treatment and heartbreaking defeats, his mind was ever active. He had faith and trust in the Lord.

Joseph knew only one direction: forward. At the time of his death he was still building Nauvoo into a major city, devoting energy to his campaign for the presidency of the United States, and organizing explorers to seek out a location in the West where the Saints could move and become a mighty people. He asked his followers to do nothing he would not do himself.

Because of his faith, the Prophet served even when it was not convenient. He also asked others who followed the Lord to serve when they were in the most trying circumstances. Brigham Young, Heber C. Kimball, and Wilford Woodruff did not find it convenient to return to Far West in fulfillment of a prophecy the Prophet made a year before, in 1839, when he was in the hands of bitter enemies. But Brigham Young would not allow a prophecy to be unfulfilled. Despite sickness among themselves and their families, and having to leave their loved ones in the most dire circumstances, the faithful apostles traveled many miles to return to Far West and then took leave for their missions. These sacrifices and manifestations of faith and obedience brought forth great blessings to the kingdom. The apostles converted many thousands in England who had been praying for the truth.

With his great faith and trust in God, Joseph had an insurmountable optimism. He knew the truth, and the truth made him free—free from fear, free from doubt, and free from pessimism. He said, "If I were sunk in the lowest pit of Nova Scotia, with the Rocky Mountains piled on me, I would hang on, exercise faith, and keep up good courage, and I would come out on top."[7]

Why was Joseph able to be cheerful, hopeful, and pleasant, and engage in fun-filled activities? He wrote:

> Now, what do we hear in the gospel which we have received? A voice of gladness! A voice of mercy from heaven; and a voice of truth out of the earth; glad tidings for the dead; a voice of gladness for the living and the dead; glad tidings of great joy. . . .

> Brethren, shall we not go on in so great a cause? Go forward and not backward. Courage, brethren; and on, on to the victory! Let your hearts rejoice, and be exceedingly glad. . . .
>
> Let the mountains shout for joy, and all ye valleys cry aloud; . . . and let all the sons of God shout for joy! (D&C 128:19, 22–23)

The Prophet loved truth. His story began with his petition for truth, which led to the First Vision. Truth made him fearless. He had a lionlike courage. He could not exchange truth for popular approval. When the people of Palmyra held a mass meeting at the time the Book of Mormon was being printed and passed a resolution against his venture, his reply was to guard the manuscript of the book more carefully.[8]

There was no retreat from truth. He published the Book of Mormon and went on to organize a church that challenged the popular errors and superstitions of the centuries.

Not only did he love truth, but he also had a remarkable ability to teach truth. Brigham Young said:

> The excellency of the glory of the character of brother Joseph Smith was that he could reduce heavenly things to the understanding of the finite. When he preached to the people—revealed the things of God, the will of God, the plan of salvation, the purposes of Jehovah, the relation in which we stand to him and all the heavenly beings, he reduced his teachings to the capacity of every man, woman, and child, making them as plain as a well-defined pathway. This should have convinced every person that ever heard of him of his divine authority and power, for no other man was able to teach as he could, and no person can reveal the things of God, but by the revelations of Jesus Christ.[9]

Elder Charles W. Penrose was impressed with the Prophet's ability to assist others in obtaining knowledge from God: "He was enabled to instruct the inhabitants of the earth how they could obtain [the Holy Ghost], . . . [so] they could obtain a knowledge of His existence through this heavenly gift, so that they might be guided in his ways and know that they were walking in his paths."[10]

Joseph was a humble man. He recognized that he was only an instrument in God's hands. He took no glory to himself. He told the Saints: "I [am] but a man, and they must not expect me to be perfect; if they expected perfection from me, I should expect it from them; but if they would bear with my infirmities and the infirmities of the brethren, I would likewise bear with their infirmities."[11]

The Prophet Joseph was completely honest. He honestly and openly made public his weaknesses. He honestly and openly expressed love. He honestly and openly expressed remorse.

Contrary to the will of the Lord, Joseph allowed Martin Harris to take the first 116 pages of the Book of Mormon manuscript that had been translated. When Martin lost them and the Lord chastised Joseph severely, Joseph made no attempt to hide his error or the Lord's rebuke. The account is in sections three and ten of the Doctrine and Covenants and is readily available for all the world to read. He did not try to hide his weaknesses. He was more concerned with helping others by example than he was with improving his own image or building his own ego.

On one occasion he characterized himself:

I am like a huge, rough stone rolling down from a high mountain; and the only polishing I get is when some corner gets rubbed off by coming in contact with something else, . . . [such as] religious bigotry, priestcraft, lawyer-craft, doctor-craft, lying editors, . . .

mobs, blasphemers, . . . and corrupt men and women—
all hell knocking off a corner here and a corner there.
Thus I will become a smooth and polished shaft in the
quiver of the Almighty, who will give me dominion
over all.[12]

The Prophet loved his fellowmen. He did not hesitate
to tell them so or to show his love by his acts. The end
of a letter to Jared Carter reads: "I love your soul, and the
souls of the children of men, and pray and do all I can for
the salvation of all."[13]

Because of his love for his fellowmen, Joseph never
missed an opportunity to preach the gospel. He was most
certainly a missionary. When he visited Washington,
D.C., he told the president of the United States about the
gospel. While in prison, he taught the gospel to guards.
Love for his fellowmen included exceedingly great love
for his family, his wife, his children, his parents, and his
brothers and sisters.

Joseph's interest in others and his concern for their
welfare was felt by nearly everybody. He enjoyed social-
izing with others. He enjoyed wrestling. Even as an adult
he frequently played catch, pulled sticks, and engaged in
similar contests with young people. He often told jokes,
to the amusement of his companions, and moved upon
the same plain as the humblest and poorest of his friends.
To him there were no strangers.[14]

Joseph had a capacity to forgive, as is displayed in a
letter he wrote to W. W. Phelps. After Brother Phelps had
signed an affidavit that led to the arrest of Joseph and
resulted in much suffering for the Saints, Joseph wrote to
him:

It is true, that we have suffered much in consequence of your behavior—the cup of gall, already full

enough for mortals to drink, was indeed filled to over-flowing when you turned against us. One with whom we had oft taken sweet counsel together, and enjoyed many refreshing seasons from the Lord—"had it been an enemy, we could have borne it." . . .

However, the cup has been drunk, the will of our Father has been done, and we are yet alive, for which we thank the Lord. . . .

. . . I shall be happy once again to give you the right hand of fellowship, and rejoice over the returning prodigal. . . .

"Come on, dear brother, since the war is past,
For friends at first, are friends again at last."[15]

Brother Phelps went on to be rebaptized and was a faithful member of the Church.

Writing in his journal in August 1842, the Prophet revealed his deep love for his wife, Emma: "With what unspeakable delight, and what transports of joy swelled my bosom, when I took by the hand, on that night, my beloved Emma—she that was my wife, even the wife of my youth, and the choice of my heart. Many were the reverberations of my mind when I contemplated for a moment the many scenes we had been called to pass through, the fatigues and the toils, the sorrows and sufferings, and the joys and consolations, from time to time, which had strewed our paths and crowned our board."[16]

Once when he was in prison for an extended time, Joseph wrote to her: "My dear Emma, I very well know your toils and sympathize with you. If God will spare my life once more to have the privilege of taking care of you, I will ease your care and endeavor to comfort your heart."[17]

Six of the eleven children of the Prophet and his wife—five natural children and one adopted son—did not survive infancy. Four natural sons and an adopted daughter lived to maturity. Emma gave birth to her last child at the age of forty, five months after the Prophet's death. He loved his children and recorded many activities with them, such as these: "After dinner I rode out in company with my wife and children." "Enjoyed myself at home with my family, all day, it being Christmas." "Remained at home and had great joy with my family."

Joseph had great love for his parents. "Words and language are inadequate to express the gratitude that I own to God for having given me so honorable a parentage," he wrote. "I love my father and his memory; and the memory of his noble deeds rests with ponderous weight upon my mind, and many of his kind and parental words to me are written on the tablet of my heart. . . . My mother also is one of the noblest and the best of all women. May God grant to prolong her days and mine, that we may live to enjoy each other's society long."[18]

Joseph's relationship with his brother Hyrum was like that of David and Jonathan: "I could pray in my heart that all my brethren were like unto my beloved brother Hyrum, who possesses the mildness of a lamb, and the integrity of a Job, and in short, the meekness and humility of Christ; and I love him with that love that is stronger than death, for I never had occasion to rebuke him, nor he me."[19]

This love and appreciation also extended to his other brothers, two of whom preceded him in death. He wrote:

"Alvin, my oldest brother—I remember well the pangs of sorrow that swelled my youthful bosom and almost burst my tender heart when he died. He was the oldest and the noblest of my father's family. He was one of the noblest of the sons of men. . . . In him there was no guile. He lived without spot from the time he was a child . . . , and when he died the angel of the Lord visited him in his last moments."[20]

"My brother Don Carlos Smith . . . also was a noble boy; I never knew any fault in him. . . . He was a lovely, a good-natured, a kind-hearted and a virtuous and a faithful, upright child; and where his soul goes, let mine go also."[21]

It seems appropriate that Joseph received revelations from God and the sealing power to assure that family life would be continued forever eternally. It must have eased the pain of separation from Alvin to know that in the future all of the Smith family could again be reunited. The Prophet Joseph has brought comfort and joy to numerous faithful who also have known the pain and heartbreak of separation from loved ones. The Lord Jesus Christ has always placed primary emphasis on the home and family, and his servant, Joseph Smith, demonstrated this in his personal behavior. Joseph did not ignore, but joyfully accepted, his responsibility as a family member.

Yes, the Prophet truly had greatness of soul. The four cornerstones of his character—faith, love of truth, humility, and love of his fellowmen—make him the epitome of the whole, well-rounded man.

NOTES

1. Leon R. Hartshorn, *Joseph Smith: Prophet of the Restoration* (Salt Lake City: Deseret Book Co., 1970), p. 38.
2. *History of the Church*, 6:468.
3. In *Journal of Discourses*, 7:176.
4. See *History of the Church*, 1:88–89.
5. "I Have a Question," *Improvement Era*, Dec. 1948, p. 809.
6. Ibid.
7. Quoted in John Henry Evans, *Joseph Smith: An American Prophet* (Salt Lake City: Deseret Book Co., 1989), p. 9.
8. See *History of the Church*, 1:76.
9. In *Journal of Discourses*, 8:206.
10. In ibid., 23:348–49.

11. *History of the Church*, 5:181.
12. Ibid., 5:401.
13. Ibid., 1:339.
14. Leonard J. Arrington, "The Human Qualities of Joseph Smith the Prophet," *Ensign*, Jan. 1971, pp. 36–37.
15. *History of the Church*, 4:163–64.
16. Ibid., 5:107.
17. James R. Clark, ed., *Messages of the First Presidency* (Salt Lake City: Bookcraft, 1965), p. 87.
18. *History of the Church*, 5:126.
19. Ibid., 2:338.
20. Ibid., 5:126.
21. Ibid., 5:127.

OH, HOW LOVELY WAS THE MORNING!

ELDER CARLOS E. ASAY

For many years the Latter-day Saints have sung with dignity and deep feeling the inspired hymn "Joseph Smith's First Prayer," written by George Manwaring. The lyrics of this sacred song describe a visible appearance of God to man that thrills the souls of all believers. Note the picturesque beauty of these words:

> Oh, how lovely was the morning!
> Radiant beamed the sun above.
> Bees were humming, sweet birds singing,
> Music ringing thru the grove,
> When within the shady woodland
> Joseph sought the God of love.
>
> . . . .
>
> Humbly kneeling, sweet appealing—
> 'Twas the boy's first uttered prayer—
> When the pow'rs of sin assailing
> Filled his soul with deep despair;
> But undaunted, still he trusted
> In his Heav'nly Father's care.

.   .   .   .

Suddenly a light descended,
Brighter far than noonday sun,
And a shining glorious pillar
O'er him fell, around him shone,
While appeared two heav'nly beings,
God the Father and the Son.

.   .   .   .

"Joseph, this is my Beloved;
Hear him!" Oh, how sweet the word!
Joseph's humble prayer was answered,
And he listened to the Lord.
Oh, what rapture filled his bosom,
For he saw the living God.
(*Hymns*, 1985, no. 26)

As described in the hymn, Joseph Smith's first vocal prayer resulted in a remarkable experience now known by millions of people as the First Vision. It was the first of many visions that the Prophet Joseph Smith received during his short ministry in mortality. It was the first in a series of events that ushered in the dispensation of the fulness of times—a time when there would be a restitution of all things spoken by all of the holy prophets since the world began (see Acts 3:18–21). It was the first of a number of spiritual occurrences that accompanied the restoration of the gospel of Jesus Christ and the establishment of "the only true and living church" (D&C 1:30). It marked the beginning of a worldwide movement destined to roll forth "until it has filled the whole earth" (D&C 65:2).

But Joseph Smith's first vision was not the first of its kind in the history of mankind. Moses saw God face to face and talked with him. In the process, Moses learned of his relationship to God, that he was a son of God, "in the similitude of [his] Only Begotten" (Moses 1:6). He learned also of the darkness of Satan and the glory of

Deity in contrast to man's present condition (see Moses 1:2–22). The Apostle Paul testified that Jesus of Nazareth appeared to him on the road to Damascus and changed the course of his life (see Acts 26:9–23). His recital of the heavenly vision prompted King Agrippa to say, "Almost thou persuadest me to be a Christian" (v. 28). Who knows how many converts Paul won during his missionary journeys after receiving his fountainhead experience? Others, such as Lehi, Nephi, and Alma, could be added to the list of privileged individuals who received marvelous manifestations of godly powers. Each vision received and recorded was glorious in its own right and was provided in accord with divine will and to fulfill divine purposes.

One might ask what divine purposes were realized by the theophany that took place in a grove near Palmyra, New York, in the spring of 1820. The full answer to this question comes only to those who understand the circumstances surrounding this singular happening. A long night of spiritual darkness, unusual religious excitement, divisions among professed Christians, ordinary farm folks seeking a greater knowledge of godly matters, and other unique conditions set the stage for the Prophet Joseph's entrance into a drama that is still being played. Among the many purposes fulfilled and the nuggets of truth drawn from the gold mine of the First Vision are these:

1. THERE ARE NO WINNERS IN WARS OF WORDS

Joseph learned that there are no winners in the tumult of opinions regarding religious matters. Such contention plays into the hands of Satan because he is the "father of contention" (3 Nephi 11:29). He is the devil who turns priest against priest and convert against convert, creating strife or engendering good feelings more pretended than real (see JS–H 1:6, 12).

Moreover, Joseph verified the fact that critical issues pertaining to the Spirit cannot be settled alone by "an appeal to the Bible" as long as teachers of religion understand the same passage of scripture so differently (JS–H 1:12).

2. SATANIC POWERS AND DARKNESS ARE REAL

Joseph learned of "the power of some actual being from the unseen world," which bound his tongue and enveloped him in thick darkness as he began to pray (JS–H 1:15–16). This power was exerted by the evil one, who viewed Joseph Smith as a threat to his realm of sin and error.

Few men have disturbed and annoyed the adversary more than Joseph did; few have felt the combined powers of darkness more than he did; and few have triumphed over Satan more nobly than he did (see JS–H 1:20).

3. POWERS OF LIGHT AND TRUTH ARE OF GOD

While praying for escape from the influence that bound his tongue and created within him a feeling of doom, Joseph learned what Moses had learned centuries before about Satan's darkness and nothingness, as compared with the light and liberty associated with God (see Moses 1:10–15). Said Joseph:

"I saw a pillar of light exactly over my head, above the brightness of the sun, which descended gradually until it fell upon me.

"It no sooner appeared than I found myself delivered from the enemy which held me bound" (JS–H 1:16–17).

"Light and truth [do] forsake [the] evil one" (D&C 93:37). The powers of darkness do flee before the powers of light, just as the night runs from the dawn.

4. THE ONLY TRUE GOD AND JESUS CHRIST APPEARED

Beholding the glorious appearance of the Father and the Son, Joseph learned that he was made in the image of God, exactly as the scriptures attest. "When the light rested upon me," Joseph recorded, "I saw two Personages, whose brightness and glory defy all description, standing above me in the air. One of them spake unto me, calling me by name and said, pointing to the other—This is My Beloved Son. Hear Him!" (JS–H 1:17).

In a matter of only a few moments, the damning myth of an impersonal, uncaring, and incomprehensible God was dispelled. The true nature of a Father in Heaven—the father of our spirits—was revealed (see Hebrews 12:9) in company with his Beloved Son, even Jesus Christ, he who had atoned for the sins of man.

Said George Q. Cannon: "But all this [the myths of Christendom] was swept away in one moment by the appearance of the Almighty Himself. . . . In one moment all this darkness disappeared, and once more there was a man found on the earth, embodied in the flesh, who had seen God, who had seen Jesus, and who could describe the personality of both."[1]

5. THE ONENESS OF THE FATHER AND THE SON IS REVEALED

Joseph learned with one glance and through few spoken words the true doctrine of the oneness of the Godhead—a doctrine that had been confused for centuries by misguided men. There appeared before him two personages who were as separate and distinct as any earthly father and son. Yet the two personages displayed a perfect unity of mind and purpose that could not be refuted. The Father expressed his love for the Son and invited him to speak, knowing that the Son would say what the Father would say if he had chosen to be voice.

Once the message was delivered, there was no need to speculate over the Savior's recorded words:

"Neither pray I for these alone, but for them also which shall believe on me through their word;

"That they all may be one; as thou, Father, art in me, and I in thee, that they also may be one in us: that the world may believe that thou hast sent me" (John 17:20–21).

6. NONE OF THE CHURCHES OF THE DAY WAS RIGHT

Joseph was instructed not to join any of the churches. He recounts:

"My object in going to inquire of the Lord was to know which of all the sects was right, that I might know which to join. No sooner, therefore, did I get possession of myself, so as to be able to speak, than I asked the Personages who stood above me in the light, which of all the sects was right . . . and which I should join.

"I was answered that I must join none of them, for they were all wrong" (JS–H 1:18–19).

This pronouncement may have troubled Joseph at first, because members of his family had affiliated with a specific faith and he had leanings toward another. But God had spoken, and who was Joseph to dispute him?

7. ERRORS OF EXISTING CHURCHES ARE EXPOSED

Joseph learned why he must not align himself with an existing church: "The Personage who addressed me said that all their creeds were an abomination in his sight; that those professors were all corrupt; that: 'they draw near to me with their lips, but their hearts are far from me, they teach for doctrines the commandments of men, having a form of godliness, but they deny the power thereof'" (JS–H 1:19).

Having seen what he had seen and having heard what he had heard, how could Joseph possibly join a sect unacceptable to the Almighty? Perhaps some of the professors were "humble followers of Christ; nevertheless, they [were] led, that in many instances they [did] err because they [were] taught by the precepts of men" (2 Nephi 28:14).

Perhaps honest efforts were being made, but whatever was being done was insufficient "to teach any man the right way" (2 Nephi 25:28).

8. THE TESTIMONY OF JAMES WAS TRUE

Joseph learned that "the testimony of James [was] true—that a man who lacked wisdom might ask of God, and obtain, and not be upbraided" (JS–H 1:26).

He also learned that a soul in the early nineteenth century was just as precious unto God as a soul in Moses' time or in the meridian of time, else why would the Lord answer his humble prayer and appear in person? Moreover, Joseph learned that personal revelation may be received by those who humble themselves and approach God with unwavering faith and with broken hearts and contrite spirits.

9. JOSEPH SMITH HAD A MISSION

Three years after his first vision, Joseph learned "that God had a work for [him] to do" and that his name should be "had for good and evil among all nations, kindreds, and tongues" (JS–H 1:33).

That declaration has been fulfilled through the publication of the Book of Mormon, the restoration of the holy priesthood, the establishment of The Church of Jesus Christ of Latter-day Saints, and the preaching of the fulness of the gospel in all the world.

10. JOSEPH BECAME A SPECIAL WITNESS FOR GOD AND HIS SON, JESUS CHRIST

Bitter persecution and reviling followed the Prophet Joseph for the rest of his life from the grove to the grave. Nonetheless, he remained true to his word and true to his special commission. Said he, "For I had seen a vision; I knew it, and I knew that God knew it, and I could not deny it" (JS–H 1:25). And at the tender age of thirty-eight and a half years, Joseph Smith died a martyr's death and sealed with his own blood his testimony—a testimony rooted in the First Vision.

These and other truths are associated with the first vision of the Prophet Joseph Smith. Each of the ten truths mentioned above constitutes a single powerful ray of living light that pierced the long night of darkness and apostasy that had held mankind in spiritual bondage for many centuries. All of the rays combined provided a floodlight of intelligence that has brought many men and women closer to God. As Orson Pratt summarized, "One minute's instruction from personages clothed with the glory of God coming down from the eternal worlds is worth more than all the volumes that ever were written by uninspired men."[2]

It all started so quietly, so simply, and so very wonderfully 175 years ago. A believing boy took one small step and prayed. A loving Father in Heaven listened and responded. What has resulted could rightfully be referred to as one giant leap for mankind.

All the towers ever built and all the spaceships ever launched pale in comparison to Joseph Smith's first vision. Though men fly higher and higher into the heavens, they will not find God or see his face unless they humble themselves, pray, and heed the truths revealed through the Prophet of the Restoration.

Some have foolishly said, "Take away Joseph Smith and his prayer in the grove and the First Vision and we can accept your message." Such people would have us bury the treasure of saving truths already cited, and many more, and turn our backs on "the most important event that had taken place in all world history from the day of Christ's ministry to the glorious hour when [the First Vision] occurred."[3]

Joseph Smith "lived great, and . . . died great in the eyes of God" (D&C 135:3). He "has done more, save Jesus only, for the salvation of men in this world, than any other man that ever lived in it" (v. 3). These words of tribute written by John Taylor, a personal friend of the Prophet Joseph and an eyewitness to the martyrdom of Joseph and Hyrum, were true when spoken and are verified each passing day as the kingdom of God goes forth so that the kingdom of heaven may come (see D&C 65:6).

Oh, how very, very lovely was the morning in the spring of 1820 when Joseph Smith sought the God of love in humble prayer! And, oh, how very wonderful it is that a caring Father in Heaven, in company with his Beloved Son, answered that prayer in the form of the First Vision! We who now bask in the light and truth that flowed from that landmark conversation between God and man owe so very much to the participants of that memorable event. It is our privilege to praise the man who communed with Jehovah, to serve the one who is the means whereby salvation comes, even Jesus Christ, and to worship in spirit and in truth God, our Father, the true and living God.

NOTES

1. In *Journal of Discourses*, 24:371–72.
2. In ibid., 12:354.
3. Bruce R. McConkie, *Mormon Doctrine*, 2nd ed. (Salt Lake City: Bookcraft, 1968), p. 285.

IN MEMORY OF THE PROPHET JOSEPH SMITH

ELDER JOE J. CHRISTENSEN

The Prophet Joseph Smith taught powerful eternal truths. I remember an experience that illustrates the point:

I taught an LDS Doctrine and Philosophy course during the summer session at the institute of religion adjacent to the University of Utah. As I became acquainted with the class members on the first day, one of the students introduced herself as a nonmember. She was a very bright and attractive third-year student majoring in history and political science, and her presence in the class helped to stimulate all of us. She asked a lot of questions and participated freely in class discussion.

Generally, things seemed to be going along well in the class. We had considered our Latter-day Saint ideas relating to the nature of God and mankind, our relationship to God, and revelation from God to man.

Then, three weeks before the summer session was to end, she stopped coming. I wondered and worried about what I might have unintentionally said that could have offended her in any way. We had no further contact until September when students were registering for the fall quarter. She called my office and arranged to come and visit for a few minutes.

When she arrived, she said, "Last summer, I registered for your course so I could find out more about what you Mormons believe. I had met a returned missionary, and we had dated a few times. He's a medical student, and I was interested in him. I decided I wanted to find out more about his beliefs in a setting where he was not present and I would feel free to ask any questions I had on my mind.

"As it turns out, all that is behind us. We are not going together anymore, and for a while that was hard for me to adjust to."

She glanced down at her handkerchief that she had wound around her fingers and continued, "I suppose you are wondering why I stopped coming to your class last summer."

I nodded, and she continued, "Well, on the first day I missed the class, as I was walking across campus toward the institute building, the thought crossed my mind, 'What if all this is true?' That thought upset me so much that I decided not to go back to class again. I would just drop the course and get away from it. I returned to my own church. I joined the choir. I even joined the civic action program sponsored by the church. I was there every Sunday and in between. I immersed myself in all the activities, but in spite of all my efforts, *the ideas would not let me go.*

"Is there something more that I could study about the Church?"

She enrolled in a Book of Mormon course and met with the missionaries. She became a member of the Church because "the ideas would not let her go." She later married and moved to the Northwest. I don't know whether she has continued to be active in the Church or not, but one thing is sure: She will never be the same. The powerful ideas of the gospel stretch our minds and spirits, and after knowing and believing even some of them, we are never the same. Yes, as Paxton wrote:

"Ideas go booming through the world louder than cannon. Thoughts are mightier than armies, and principles have achieved more victories than horsemen or chariots."

These powerful gospel principles have come to us through the Prophet Joseph Smith and the restoration to the earth of The Church of Jesus Christ of Latter-day Saints.

Even though he was blessed with many talents and capacities, Joseph Smith could not have accomplished what he did without divine help. Of that I bear solemn testimony, and I hope that anyone who has not as yet had the incentive to read and evaluate Joseph Smith's life and mission will do so. If you do, I am confident that you will come to a similar conclusion.

To both members and nonmembers of The Church of Jesus Christ of Latter-day Saints, I assure you that there is much in the life of Joseph Smith that is worthy of our most serious thought. Pondering his life and his teachings can bring intellectual satisfaction, motivation to improve one's life, a meaningful understanding of who we are and how we relate to all that is around us in the world, and, most of all, a deep spiritual commitment to our Savior, Jesus the Christ.

The angel Moroni appeared to Joseph Smith on 21 September 1823. Joseph said of this visit:

"He called me by name, and said . . . that God had a work for me to do; and that my name should be had for good and evil among all nations, kindreds, and tongues, or that it should be both good and evil spoken of among all people" (JS–H 1:33).

This is a most remarkable prophecy! Any one of us could say that our names would be had for good and evil among all nations and it simply would not happen. Most of us will not be known outside of the immediate area where we live.

There was much evil spoken of the Prophet and much evil done to him and those who believed in his message. Although most of you likely have heard the account describing the situation that existed in the jail in Richmond, Missouri, on a wintry November night in 1838, I would like to recount it again here. I invite your empathy. Put yourself in the situation and be reminded of one of the difficulties through which the Prophet went and how he reacted to it. In the words of Parley P. Pratt:

> In one of those tedious nights we had lain as if in sleep till the hour of midnight had passed, and our ears and hearts had been pained, while we had listened for hours to the obscene jests, the horrid oaths, the dreadful blasphemies and filthy language of our guards, Colonel Price at their head, as they recounted to each other their deeds of rapine, murder, robbery, etc., which they had committed among the "*Mormons*" while at Far West and vicinity. They even boasted of defiling by force wives, daughters and virgins, and of shooting or dashing out the brains of men, women and children.
>
> I had listened till I became so disgusted, shocked, horrified, and so filled with the spirit of indignant jus-

tice that I could scarcely refrain from rising upon my feet and rebuking the guards; but had said nothing to Joseph, or any one else, although I lay next to him and knew he was awake. On a sudden he arose to his feet, and spoke in a voice of thunder, or as the roaring lion, uttering, as near as I can recollect, the following words:

"SILENCE, ye fiends of the infernal pit. In the name of Jesus Christ I rebuke you, and command you to be still; I will not live another minute and hear such language. Cease such talk, or you or I die THIS INSTANT!"

He ceased to speak. He stood erect in terrible majesty. Chained, and without a weapon; calm, unruffled and dignified as an angel, he looked upon the quailing guards, whose weapons were lowered or dropped to the ground; whose knees smote together, and who, shrinking into a corner, or crouching at his feet, begged his pardon, and remained quiet till a change of guards.

I have seen the ministers of justice, clothed in magisterial robes, and criminals arraigned before them, while life was suspended on a breath, in the Courts of England; I have witnessed a Congress in solemn session to give laws to nations; I have tried to conceive of kings, of royal courts, of thrones and crowns; and of emperors assembled to decide the fate of kingdoms; but dignity and majesty have I seen but *once*, as it stood in chains, at midnight, in a dungeon in an obscure village of Missouri.[1]

Almost from the beginning, Joseph Smith's name was vilified. Evil was spoken of him by the vast majority of those around him. He was attacked verbally and even physically by those who should at least have given him the common human courtesy of tolerant patience. After he told others of his remarkable experience in the grove, many began charging that he was lazy, indolent, uneducated, opportunistic, psychologically unbalanced, lecherous, heretical, blasphemous, and the list goes on and on. Indeed, evil has been spoken of him in the past, and there are those today who continue to do so.

But Joseph Smith, who died at the young age of thirty-eight, did "more, save Jesus only, for the salvation of men in this world, than any other man that ever lived in it" (D&C 135:3). This tribute, written by John Taylor shortly after the Prophet's death, has been supported by the testimonies of many others whose lives have been changed for the better by the work of Joseph Smith.

One of the greatest aspects of Joseph Smith's ministry was the continuous flow of revelation that came through him to become scripture. President Stephen L Richards said the following about the literary contributions of Joseph Smith:

> His literary labors must not be forgotten. He produced more scripture, that is, the revealed word of God, than any other man of whom we have record. Indeed, his total scriptural productions would almost equal those of all others put together. Within the pages of the Book of Mormon, the Doctrine and Covenants and the Pearl of Great Price, which came to the world through him, are to be found such truth gems as, "The glory of God is intelligence"; "Men are that they might have joy"; it is the work and the glory of God to bring to pass the immortality and eternal life of man; and a clear statement of the purpose of good and evil in the world—a philosophical problem which has baffled the scholars of all times—and many other truths of inestimable value. There also came from him such memorable sayings as, "It is impossible for a man to be saved in ignorance"; "A man is saved no faster than he gets knowledge"; "Whatever principle of intelligence we attain unto in this life it will rise with us in the resurrection." He wrote history and dissertations on many

subjects and was an orator of magnetism and convincing force.

The world's enlightenment of the century following his life has not disclosed a single error in his theological and philosophical pronouncements, and the society which he established is without question the peer, and many students not belonging to it maintain it is the superior, of all social systems on the earth.[2]

One of the Church's modern-day scholars, Dr. Truman Madsen, who has dedicated a good share of his life to a study of the philosophy and contributions of Joseph Smith, wrote:

> [Joseph Smith's] Biblical teachings, letters and counsels are so extensive as to transcend the grasp of any one historian. . . .
>
> *Philosophically*, though neither schooled nor skilled in Western thought, he spoke profoundly of eternal law, of the ultimate elements of the cosmos, of the relationship of matter and spirit, of space and time, of the nature of freedom, of causation and process, of the meaning and unity of truth, of the foundations of ethics, and of history, education and languages.
>
> *Theologically*, without bookish erudition, he testified first-hand of the revealed personalities of God and Jesus Christ, the origins of man, including his pre-existence, the meaning of becoming sons of God in the fullest sense, the events of Eden, the reality of angels and spirits, the powers of opposition, the problem of evil, the nature of resurrection. Under these insights a host of traditional paradoxes dissolve.
>
> *Religiously*, he searched the inner life, taught of the roots of man's anguish and guilt, the sanctifying "powers of godliness" that emanate from Jesus Christ, and unfold man's intelligence, quicken his spirit, and heal his very blood stream. He taught of the light of God, its sources and effects. He manifested such grasp of the

meaning of life as to exceed, even, the aspirations of men of faith in every age.

All this came "line by line," "here a little and there a little." Yet it has been noted that it is remarkably coherent, both with itself, and with the combined experiences of those who have taken it seriously. That it could have come from, or even through, a mind as taxed by a thousand other matters as was Joseph Smith's, staggers the imagination. (He was in his grave at half the age of most ranking theologians.)[3]

All this was accomplished while Joseph Smith lived in and was forced out of four states: New York, Ohio, Missouri, and Illinois, where he was martyred. In the process he was often a fugitive, he was harassed by more than forty lawsuits, and he had the emotional and temporal concerns of a young husband and father of nine children, of whom five were buried along the way.

Let's consider a few of the statements about Joseph Smith that have been made by scholars and theologians illustrating that his name is also being had for good. The great Russian statesman, author, and philosopher Count Leo Nikolaevich Tolstoi had a very high opinion of the work of the Prophet Joseph Smith, as indicated in the account of his conversation about a century ago with Dr. Andrew D. White, former president of Cornell University and U.S. foreign minister to Russia:

> "Dr. White," said Count Tolstoi, "I wish you would tell me about your American religion."
>
> "We have no state church in America," replied Dr. White.
>
> "I know that, but what about your American religion?"
>
> Patiently then Dr. White explained to the Count that in America there are many religions, and that each

person is free to belong to the particular church in which he is interested.

To this Tolstoi impatiently replied: "I know all of this, but I want to know about the *American* religion. Catholicism originated in Rome; the Episcopal Church originated in England; the Lutheran Church in Germany, but the Church to which I refer originated in America, and is commonly known as the Mormon Church. What can you tell me of the teachings of the Mormons?"

"Well," said Dr. White, "I know very little concerning them. They have an unsavory reputation, they practice polygamy, and are very superstitious."

Then Count Leo Tolstoi, in his honest and stern, but lovable manner, rebuked the ambassador. "Dr. White, I am greatly surprised and disappointed that a man of your great learning and position should be so ignorant on this important subject. The Mormon people teach the American religion; their principles teach the people not only of Heaven and its attendant glories, but how to live so that their social and economic relations with each other are placed on a sound basis. If the people follow the teachings of this Church, nothing can stop their progress—it will be limitless. There have been great movements started in the past but they have died or been modified before they reached maturity. If Mormonism is able to endure, unmodified, until it reaches the third and fourth generations, it is destined to become the greatest power the world has ever known."[4]

Dr. Harold Bloom, a distinguished professor of humanities at Yale University, published his book *The American Religion* in 1992. He included several chapters dealing with the work of Joseph Smith. Although I do *not* agree with many of his conclusions, I certainly agree with several of his statements lauding the Prophet, such as the following:

"Whatever his lapses, Smith was an authentic religious genius, unique in our national history."[5]

"I also do not find it possible to doubt that Joseph Smith was an authentic prophet. Where in all of American history can we find his match? . . . In proportion to his importance and his complexity, *[Joseph Smith] remains the least-studied personage, of an undiminished vitality, in our entire national saga.*"[6]

"If there is already in place any authentic version of the American Religion then, as Tolstoy surmised, it must be Mormonism, whose future as yet may prove decisive for the nation, and for more than this nation alone."[7]

Jesuit scholar Gustave Weigel wrote of Joseph Smith: "His productivity marks him as a man of genius. He had very little schooling, possessing only the knowledge of the three R's, and yet he was a combination of practical wisdom, great daring and rich imagination."[8]

Heikki Raisanen, a Finnish theologian writing in German, commented on the Prophet's work and pointed out that "Joseph's teachings provide solutions for most, if not all, of the genuine problems and contradictions of the Bible with which scholars have wrestled for generations."[9]

In an article on Raisanen, Edwin Haroldsen discusses Raisanen's opinions about one of the difficult questions that has confounded theologians for centuries:

> How can we say that God has an eternal plan of salvation when, according to traditional Christian theology, Jesus Christ brought a new way of salvation which the ancients did not know? Did earlier generations actually know the divine plan of salvation, or did God mislead them by giving them a law that was both preparatory and transitory? If, however, the ancients could, in fact, be saved by the law they knew, what

was the need for Jesus Christ? Did God think of a better plan after his first one failed?

Mr. Raisanen wrote that the Prophet Joseph Smith's answer to these questions—that Jesus Christ carried out a single divine plan of salvation, a plan known by the ancient prophets—*was to him a thing of "pure logic and downright beauty."*

The Finnish theologian concluded with a plea for scholars no longer to dismiss Joseph Smith's statements out of hand, but to study them on the basis of "objective, scholarly considerations."[10]

The powerful ideas taught by the Prophet satisfy the most inquiring mind. A study conducted by the Princeton Religion Research Center indicates that among Americans generally, those with more formal education are not as active in their churches as those with less education.[11] There is some good evidence that the ideas contained within The Church of Jesus Christ of Latter-day Saints apparently provide such meaningful answers to the questions faced by university students that the ratio of church activity is higher among Latter-day Saints who have the most formal education. A survey among several thousand members indicated that 78 percent of the members who are college graduates attend Church regularly compared with only 49 percent of those with only a high school education. Seventy-two percent of college graduates are tithe payers compared with 46 percent who have only a high school education.[12]

I had an experience that illustrates this situation: In the early sixties, I served as a member of the Association of Directors of Religion at a university in the Northwest. A broad variety of faiths was represented in the group. We met monthly in a seminar room to discuss common concerns about our assignments with the university students of our particular faiths.

One Monday morning before the meeting had formally begun, I was seated to the left of one of the ministers. He leaned back in his chair with his hands clasped behind his head. In a pensive and somewhat anxious mood, he shared in his typical manner of expression a concern and question: "It seems to me that in the evolutionary development of college-age religiosity, we have come to a time when it is no longer considered relevant by university students to attend Sunday evening church services." (In other words, attendance among his group was falling off.)

He turned to his right, and asked, "How do you find it in your group?" The ministers began to respond one after another. One of the first nodded in agreement. Another said that the liturgy (or written worship service) of his church was not considered relevant by the college-age members and should be modernized so that it would "speak to them" and keep them actively participating. Each in his own way agreed that, over time, the involvement in their groups was decreasing.

Finally, since each around the circle had commented, it came my turn as the last to respond. At the time, I was also serving as the bishop of the student ward. The Sunday evening before this Monday meeting of directors of religion, I had received a note from Brother Huber, our ward clerk. It was handed to me during sacrament meeting, which is our Sunday evening worship service. It contained the following message: "Congratulations, Bishop! Tonight we have the highest sacrament meeting attendance we have had since we were called to serve." Our experience was just the opposite of all who had responded. The attendance of the Latter-day Saint university students was steadily increasing. I tried to select a way to report that to the group as humbly as possible.

Among university-age students that are members, as well as other members of The Church of Jesus Christ of Latter-day Saints, activity levels and affirmative identity are growing. They are even higher today than they were in the 1960s. I am convinced that one powerful reason is found in the truths that have been restored through the Prophet Joseph Smith.

Another impressive illustration of the power of these Restoration ideas happened a number of years ago when I received an invitation to represent our church in a Religion in Life Conference at one of the universities in the Southwest. Two individuals were invited each year to represent their particular religion. The year I went, they had invited representatives from the Mormons and the Moslems. I suppose they had an alphabetical listing and our church appeared by the nickname. As I remember, the Moslem representative was a doctoral candidate studying at the University of Illinois.

The next three days were very busy. I was involved in making twenty-two presentations to classes, large groups, small groups, and faculty members. One of the presentations was to a philosophy class, which met in the evenings for two hours. It was located in one of the science buildings in an amphitheater-like lecture room with a long laboratory table stretched across the front.

My wife, Barbara, and I and our student host arrived a few minutes before the class was to begin. I had no idea who was teaching the class or what his or her attitude might be toward institutionalized religion. The professor met us outside the door and basically said, "Now when you get in there, I don't want you to take the time telling the students about all the ways your church is like other churches. I want you to take the first hour and a half telling them how your church is different from other Christian churches."

Then he added with a twinkle in his eye, "And I want you to tell them in such a way that you will make Mormons out of all of them!"

What I interpreted this to mean was that I was to speak from my heart and not feel any problem with telling them what I believed.

He opened the door and ushered us into the classroom where about eighty-five students were seated. I was hurriedly outlining in my mind some of the ideas that make our faith distinctive from traditional Christian faiths. (If you had received that assignment, what would you have included?)

During the next hour and a half, I shared with them some of the great ideas we have received in the doctrine and theology of the Church as restored through the Prophet Joseph Smith, including the nature of God, the nature of man, our relationship to our Father in Heaven and Jesus Christ, the Creation, the problem of evil, continuous revelation, a lay priesthood, and eternal progression.

At the conclusion of thirty minutes of good, searching questions and responses, the class ended. I stood near the exit and was speaking with a few students who wanted to ask additional questions. After a few minutes, the professor approached me and said, pointing to the student host, who was a returned missionary, "That fellow over there said that you believe this." He had written in shorthand some notes on a pad and read through them:

"'As man is God once was, and as God is man may become.' Do you believe that?"

I had purposely *not* used that statement during my remarks to the class because I felt that I could raise more dust with that one than I would be able to settle in one class period. I didn't have any idea whether the professor thought the idea was good, bad, or indifferent. I said that the statement came from Lorenzo Snow in the 1830s and explained that as a result of scripture and latter-day revelation, we know a lot more about what God is like now than what He may have been like before. Then, after circumlocuting around and around the question, I finally said, "Yes, we believe that."

He looked down at his notes and slowly and pensively mumbled through the words again: "As man is God once was, and as God is man may become."

"Hmmmm . . . " Then with genuine enthusiasm, he said, "That is the *greatest* idea I have ever heard!"

He was elated. He made his living teaching ideas, and the greatest idea he had ever heard came through the Prophet Joseph Smith.

During my years of graduate school, I was exposed to a lot of psychological and philosophical thought, and if I had taken some of it seriously, my testimony would not have been strengthened. One of my professors, who had been educated in schools and a university sponsored by his church, had become "emancipated," or freed, from institutionalized religion, and he would have been pleased if his students would have done the same. Freud and other influential thinkers and writers have concluded that religion is a manmade illusion and that from primitive times to the present, man has created gods in his own image. These anthropomorphic gods have become for them father figures, or crutches for those who are still mentally dependent.[13]

I think it would be interesting to spend some time studying such topics as the strength of our position in believing in theomorphic man, or man with a body like God's or created in the image of God as we read in Genesis, as opposed to a belief in an anthropomorphic god, or a god created in the image of man. There is a powerful difference between those two concepts. Also, it would be interesting to consider the power that comes from a belief in eternalism, as our church has defined it, in contrast to the belief taught in most Christian churches that God is the *only* eternal and, consequently, everything that exists was created *ex nihilo,* or out of nothing. Through the restoration of the gospel, we have meaningful answers to the age-old philosophical problem of evil and the origin of the sin, sickness, suffering, and catastrophes we see in the world. Thanks to the Prophet Joseph Smith, we don't have to blame God for all that exists because there are other eternals, including the elements, polar forces, priesthood, and truth. Because of the eternals of our own intelligence and agency, we as human beings must take responsibility for much of the evil that exists in the world. We can neither blame God, nor can we merely say that "the devil made me do it."

We should be especially grateful for the powerful answers to the great philosophical questions of the ages that have come to us through the Prophet Joseph Smith and the restoration of the gospel in our times.

President Brigham Young said: "I feel like shouting hallelujah, all the time, when I think that I ever knew Joseph Smith, the Prophet whom the Lord raised up and ordained, and to whom He gave keys and power to build up the kingdom of God on earth and sustain it."[14]

I also feel like shouting hallelujah all the time when I think that I ever had the privilege of knowing even a portion of the powerful ideas revealed through Joseph Smith the Prophet.

I have tried to remember when I first came to know that Joseph Smith was a prophet of God. I searched my memory and finally concluded that I can't recall when I didn't know that he was a prophet. This knowledge seems to have always been a part of me. My testimony of the Prophet is one of my most valuable possessions, for which I will be eternally grateful. Over the years I have read many accounts of apostates and anti-Mormons who have written negative things about him. Still the deep conviction continues to grow within me that Joseph Smith in very deed was a prophet of the Lord.

Although my acquaintance with the Prophet Joseph was not personal, I resonate to John Taylor's "Affidavit," written after the martyrdom and based on his personal association with Joseph Smith. He wrote:

> I testify that I was acquainted with Joseph Smith for years. I have traveled with him; I have been with him in private and in public; I have associated with him in councils of all kinds; I have listened hundreds of times to his public teachings, and his advice to his friends and associates of a more private nature. I have been at his house and seen his deportment in his family. I have seen him arraigned before the tribunals of his country, and have seen him honorably acquitted, and delivered from the pernicious breath of slander, and the machinations and falsehoods of wicked and corrupt men. I was with him living, and with him when he died, when he was murdered in Carthage jail by a ruthless mob . . . with their faces painted. I was there and was myself wounded; I at that time received four balls in my body. I have seen him, then, under these various circumstances, and I testify before God, angels, and men, that he was a good, honorable, virtuous man— that his doctrines were good, scriptural, and whole-

some—that his precepts were such as became a man of God—that his private and public character was un-impeachable—and that he lived and died as a man of God and a gentleman. This is my testimony. If it is disputed, bring me a person authorized to receive an affidavit, and I will make one to this effect. I therefore testify of things which I know and of things which I have seen.[15]

John Taylor said about Joseph Smith's intelligence:

God chose this young man. He was ignorant of letters as the world has it, but the most profoundly learned and intelligent man that I ever met in my life, and I have traveled hundreds of thousands of miles, been on different continents and mingled among all classes and creeds of people, yet I have never met a man so intelligent as he was.[16]

About his character:

We hear about Joseph Smith's crimes. He was tried thirty-nine times before the tribunals of his country, and nothing proved against him. Why do not these gentlemen bring some legal, authenticated testimony from those courts? Why did not the authors of these books do this? Because they could not.

As they cannot overturn his principles, they attack his character. And that is one reason why we have so many books written against his character, without touching his principles, and also why we meet with so much opposition. But truth, eternal truth, is invulnerable. It cannot be destroyed, but like the throne of Jehovah, it will outride all the storms of men, and live for ever.[17]

About the truths that Joseph Smith taught:

Suppose Joseph Smith was all you represent him to be—your systems are still as unscriptural. And the next thing you will have to do will be to prove the scriptures false, if you would sustain them. The eternal truths of God are still the same, and whether Joseph Smith was a good or a bad man, the truths we preach are scriptural, and you cannot gainsay them; and if they are, what avails your attack upon character? Your soporiferous draughts may lull the people to sleep for a while, but truth will roll forth. The honest in heart will be aroused from their slumber. The purposes of God will roll forth. The kingdom of God will be established, and in spite of your puny efforts, truth will stand proud and erect, unsullied and uncontaminated by the pestiferous breath of calumniating mortals, and no power can stay its progress.[18]

Now what does this mean for us? Here are a few suggestions:

First, we should study more about the prophet.

No one has yet plumbed the depths of what could be learned about his life or teachings. We should commit ourselves to thoughtful study and consideration.

Second, and of greater importance, we should strive to incorporate into our lives the principles that he taught, which can bring us all the blessings that President Stephen L Richards describes:

> If any man has received in his heart the witness of the divine truth embraced in the contributions of the Prophet Joseph, I charge him to be true,—true to his testimony, true to the Prophet, the founder, true to the cause and its duly commissioned leaders, true to the covenants he has made in holy places, and true to the brotherhood of man in the service that he renders. If any man has not received this witness, I appeal for his thoughtful, prayerful, sympathetic consideration. I offer to him, out of the experience of my life, a humble but certain assurance that if he will receive and apply the teachings of Joseph Smith he will be made happy.

Doubt and uncertainty will leave him. Glorious purpose will come into life. Family ties will be sweeter.
Friendships will be dearer. Service will be nobler, and
the peace of Christ will be his portion. I so testify in
the name of Jesus Christ, amen.[19]

Permit me to repeat again those promises: "If he will
receive and apply the teachings of Joseph Smith he will
be made happy. Doubt and uncertainty will leave him.
Glorious purpose will come into life. Family ties will be
sweeter. Friendships will be dearer. Service will be
nobler, and the peace of Christ will be his portion."

I concur completely with this testimony.

Joseph Smith wrote about the future of the Church in
1842 as part of the Wentworth letter to the editor of the
Chicago Democrat newspaper: "Our missionaries are
going forth to different nations, and . . . the Standard of
Truth has been erected; no unhallowed hand can stop the
work from progressing; persecutions may rage, mobs may
combine, armies may assemble, calumny may defame,
but the truth of God will go forth boldly, nobly, and inde-
pendent, till it has penetrated every continent, visited
every clime, swept every country, and sounded in every
ear, till the purposes of God shall be accomplished, and
the great Jehovah shall say the work is done."[20]

The Church of Jesus Christ of Latter-day Saints is
growing rapidly throughout the world, including in coun-
tries behind the former iron curtain. Whoever would
have dreamed that we would live long enough to see the
day! If Dr. Rodney Stark's predictions are correct and the
Church's growth trends continue, there will be 265 million members of the Church by the year 2080.[21]

Of the Church, Dr. Stark said: "We are observing
an extraordinarily rare event. After a hiatus of fourteen

hundred years, in our time a new world faith seems to be stirring."[22]

The prediction of Count Leo Tolstoi may more completely be realized: The Church will literally have become the greatest power the world has ever known.

And so it shall be. With or without you and me, it shall go forth. But it will go forth a lot better with us than without us!

May we come to the realization that indeed "Joseph Smith, the Prophet and Seer of the Lord, has done more, save Jesus only, for the salvation of men in this world, than any other man that ever lived in it" (D&C 135:3).

I testify that Joseph Smith was truly a prophet of the Lord Jesus Christ. Through him we know great truths about our Father in Heaven and his great plan of happiness, which brings supernal meaning into our lives forever. I will be eternally grateful for all the gifts our Father in Heaven has given us through the Prophet Joseph Smith.

NOTES

1. *Autobiography of Parley P. Pratt* (Salt Lake City: Deseret Book Co., 1938), pp. 210–11.
2. *Contributions of Joseph Smith* (pamphlet, 1958), p. 7.
3. *Joseph Smith among the Prophets* (The New England Mission of The Church of Jesus Christ of Latter-day Saints, 1963), pp. 5–6.
4. Quoted in LeGrand Richards, *A Marvelous Work and a Wonder*, rev. ed. (Salt Lake City: Deseret Book Co., 1973), pp. 435–36.
5. *The American Religion* (New York: Simon and Schuster, 1992), p. 82.
6. Ibid, p. 95; emphasis added.
7. Ibid, p. 97.
8. *Churches in North America: An Introduction* (New York: Schocken Books, 1965), p. 90.
9. Quoted in Edwin O. Haroldsen, "Good and Evil Spoken Of," published in *Ensign* (Aug. 1995, pp. 8–11) in a version different from the original article in which this quotation appears.

10. Quoted in "Good and Evil Spoken Of," *Ensign*, Aug. 1995, p. 10; emphasis added; original article by Heikki Raisanen titled "Joseph Smith und die Bibel: Die Leistung des mormonischen Propheten in neuer Beleuchtung," *Theologische Literaturzeitung*, Feb. 1984, pp. 83–92.
11. See study published in 1982.
12. See a survey of more than 7,000 LDS adults in the U.S. and Canada (Research Division, LDS Church, 1981).
13. See Sigmund Freud, *The Future of an Illusion*, as one example.
14. In *Journal of Discourses*, 3:51.
15. *The Gospel Kingdom*, sel. G. Homer Durham (Salt Lake City: Deseret Book Co., 1943), p. 355.
16. In *Journal of Discourses*, 21:163.
17. *Gospel Kingdom*, pp. 355–56.
18. Ibid, p. 356.
19. *Contributions of Joseph Smith*, p. 9.
20. *History of the Church*, 4:540.
21. "Modernization and Mormon Growth," in *Contemporary Mormonism: Social Science Perspectives*, ed. Marie Cornwall et al. (Urbana, Ill.: University of Illinois, 1994).
22. "Rise of a New World Faith," *Review of Religious Research* 26 (1984): 118–27.

CHRISTIANITY AND THE HOPE OF THE FUTURE

ELDER F. ENZIO BUSCHE

The other day I was watching a news broadcast on local television. A Protestant minister stated bluntly that Mormons cannot be considered Christians. As I pondered this statement, my thoughts went back to the history of the Christian world and several age-old questions that always are new: What is truth? Who is qualified or authorized to make judgment? Who truly represents the Lord and teaches his plan of salvation on this earth?

These questions obviously are most significant. The Lord, Jesus Christ, during His earthly ministry, made the statement, "I am the way, the truth, and the life: no man cometh unto the Father, but by me" (John 14:6). In His foreknowledge, Christ must have seen what would happen to coming generations before He would restore His kingdom on this earth. He gave His disciples a profound warning: "Beware of false prophets, which come to you in sheep's clothing, but inwardly they are ravening wolves" (Matthew 7:15). He then explained how to find and identify His disciples:

Ye shall know them by their fruits. Do men gather grapes of thorns, or figs of thistles?

Even so every good tree bringeth forth good fruit; but a corrupt tree bringeth forth evil fruit. . . .

Every tree that bringeth not forth good fruit is hewn down, and cast into the fire.

Wherefore by their fruits ye shall know them. (Matthew 7:16–20)

Because some ministers of traditional churches want to deny us the right to be called Christian, I feel that we should look into the history of Christianity for clues to identify the fruit we should be seeking. I invite you, therefore, to join me in a short review of Christian history. This review not only will help us identify the fruit we should be seeking, but perhaps also will help us find the roots of the misery that challenges the very existence of mankind in our day.

When we look into the heritage of our Western culture, we cannot separate political history from the history of the Christian churches. The two histories are connected and interwoven inseparably. As we dare to look back and study the development of the Christian churches and nations over a period of nearly two thousand years, we understand that the wonderful message of Christ, "Glory to God in the highest, and on earth peace, good will toward men" (Luke 2:14), has never been fulfilled.

In fact, this scripture appears to be further from being fulfilled now than ever before. Even though we are not engaged now in another full-scale war, a complete loss of the fabric of a peaceful society in nearly all nations overshadows mankind.

Looking at the roots of past wars and the civil unrest spreading through the nations in our day, the one reason for all of them is apparent: The people of the world, including the so-called Christian world, refuse to pursue or even accept the first and great commandment of Christ: to love the Lord our God with all our hearts, and with all our souls, and with all our minds, and to love our neighbors as ourselves (see Matthew 22:37–39).

The absence of this principle of love and the obvious refusal to believe in this divine commandment, even the perversion of it by giving it lip service, find roots in the very beginnings of Christian churches. Because of a flood of old documents that have been discovered in many places in our day, the roots of Christian churches are hidden no longer in dark clouds of mystery. These roots no longer are subject to the exclusive interpretation of rulers in power.

In pursuing our investigation, we can make certain statements that illustrate dramatically the dilemma in which the world, especially the Christian world, finds itself today. For instance, I draw your attention to the fact that today's historians suggest that the early disciples of Christ believed He would return very soon. Therefore, they did not write in detail any reports of His life for a period of one generation.

According to Karl Maly, a Catholic historian, not until A.D. 70 was the first attempt made to write the words and deeds of Jesus as a testimony and as a reason for Christian belief.[1] Alfons Kemmer, another Catholic historian, wrote that in the second half of the first century, the first writings of the Savior's disciples, the apostles, appeared. He mentioned that the complete list of the twenty-seven books that now comprise the canonical New Testament can be found for the first time in a letter by Bishop Athanasius of Alexandria in A.D. 367 Kemmer also pointed out that the development of an understanding as to which documents were generally accepted as divinely inspired and, therefore, canonical was not concluded until the famous Council of Trent in A.D. 1546.[2]

Historians of our time leave no question that in the very early days of the development of Christian churches, so-called Christians disputed without end about the validity and authenticity of manuscripts, words, and interpretations. It seems that because of this background, the lay member of the Catholic church was, for many centuries, not given personal access to the scriptures. It took the churches of the Reformation to give to the individual member access to the Bible with the accompanying understanding that the Bible was flawless as to doctrine and authority. As mentioned before, a mass of old and new manuscripts has been found in our day. They shed more light on the fact that, from the very beginning of the Christian church, many different movements existed that were heretical or were called heretical by the established groups. We now understand that even the so-called canonical scriptures were established only amidst bitter contention.[3]

According to Maly, in the groundswell of the awakening movement of historical science in the beginning of the nineteenth century, intensive exploration of the Bible's origin brought the awareness that one has to understand the Bible as a document of a certain time in which language and imaginations were geared towards the needs of that period. In order to understand, it would be necessary to see the Bible in the perspective of the background of its time.[4] A critical analysis started with the awareness that all autographed books of the text had disappeared. However, newly found New Testament manuscripts dated from the third to the eighteenth century include the following: 2,000 manuscripts of the four gospels; 400 manuscripts of Acts and the Pauline and Catholic letters together; and 300 manuscripts of Pauline letters.

Study of the manuscripts has shown that 150,000 textual variations are obvious. Even all available copies that precede the printing press in the fifteenth century show textual variations. The manuscripts show clearly that no punctuation, no accents, and no breathing marks were included to help the translators.[5]

The intense discussions and the number of new Bible translations by various translators and various churches in recent years finally compelled even the Catholic church to reevaluate its position. According to Alfons Kemmer, at the second Vatican Council called in November 1962, the so-called "battle of the Bible" arose. A minority wanted to hold rigidly to the old teaching from St. Augustine that the Bible is flawless and all-inclusive. However, during the third and fourth periods of the Vatican Council in 1964 and 1965, and after extensive debate, the Catholic church reached a compromise in a synthesis of traditional Bible understanding and modern Bible science. As a result, the second Vatican Council authorized a totally new translation of the Bible for the Catholic church.[6]

Different opinions about the question "What is the established truth?" arose very early in Christian history. The followers of various gnostic groups, who were widespread in the Roman empire for many centuries, emphasized the need for spiritual knowledge of truth and emphasized that such knowledge is essential for salvation.[7] The followers of Marcion (who died in A.D. 160) stressed the necessity for humans to develop charity as the Lord's saving power.[8] The Montanists, at the end of the second century, stressed the need for self-discipline. Their women, for instance, were required to wear veils.[9]

Because I cannot mention all of the various groups and developments in this brief summary, I will concentrate on some of the most important and more interesting ones.

The followers of Origenes (who died in A.D. 254) believed that to be a disciple of Christ, a person must be an example in deed, in language, and in daily behavior.[10]

Arius, who lived in the days of the Council of Nice and who converted multitudes to Christianity, believed the Father and the Son to be two different personages. This belief contrasted with the Nicene Creed.[11]

In A.D. 418 Pelagius, a Roman citizen of British origin, taught that the children of God have free agency. This teaching clashed with the prevailing predestination teaching of Augustine.[12]

Later, when Christianity had spread over the entire western European continent and the Catholic church was established as the dominant Christian church, many people and groups still claimed to be inspired. They were in open opposition to the established church. The Cathari, for instance, did not believe in worshiping the bones of early Christian martyrs. They tried to take the scriptures seriously.[13] This group became prominent in the tenth century. Peter Waldo, who lived in Lyons, France, led another group. He believed that a priest of the Lord should be righteous and should have high standards of morality.[14] In the fourteenth century, the Begins and the Begards originated in Germany. They believed that a man can become perfect when he strives to receive the gifts of the Spirit.[15] Also originating in the fourteenth century in Germany were the Salpeterer, who believed that worldly power and church power should be separated.[16]

John Wycliffe from England and John Huss from Bohemia were immediate forerunners of the Reformation. Finally, Martin Luther, Huldreich Zwingli, and John Calvin led the Reformation. But the Reformation did not bring a united, new understanding of truth. On the contrary, it only opened many new interpretations, new understandings, and, of course, new disputes.

For instance, Thomas Muenzer asked to separate the church from the state. He developed a movement of awareness among desperate, exploited, and suppressed peasants.

Some others were inspired to establish a city they called New Jerusalem. They refused to believe in the baptism of small children and, therefore, were called Anabaptists.[17] They were the early forerunners of the present-day Baptists.

From the Reformation in England came the Puritans. They wanted to confine themselves to the pure contents of the gospel. They became the founding fathers of the Presbyterians, the Congregationalists, and some of the Reformed churches.[18]

We have considered only major developments in how Christian belief has been interpreted. However, I believe I can make my first statement without contradiction: *The message of Christ and His gospel became subject, soon after His resurrection, to extremely controversial interpretations. Also, the question "What is truth?" continues to be controversial to this day.*

When we investigate another aspect of the history of Christian churches, we see that modern historians have reached an astonishing conclusion. They have concluded that present-day Christianity is the result of gospel interpretations made by those who were strong enough to suppress differing opinions.

During the first centuries after the resurrection of the Savior, a conflict raged over which interpretations were right and over the true requirements for salvation. It was ended by force after the Council of Nice. The Roman Emperor Constantine called selected Christian bishops to the council in A.D. 325. Regarding this council, the Catholic historian Karl Kupisch wrote:

> Of the 4,000 bishops, only 250 came. From all of western Europe only four bishops were present. The bishop from Rome was not present. Constantine did not subject himself to be questioned. He was the master of the conference. His ideas and his concepts were accepted.[19]

According to this same author, the Nicene Creed became the law of the Roman empire. Orthodox Christianity became an essential qualification for Roman citizenship. The Roman emperor wanted unity among his various provinces. He used Christianity as the tool to establish this unity by force. The Christians, who had been persecuted during the first centuries after the resurrection of Christ, now became the oppressors, paired with the power of the Roman empire.

With the coronation of the Germanic Frankish King Charlemagne in A.D. 800 as the emperor of the Roman empire, the secular empire was declared identical with the state of God (*civitas dei*), and the emperor understood himself in theory and practice to be God's representative. From that time on, the empire was called the "Holy" Roman Empire. It may be permitted to mention that the German historian Rudolph Wahl wrote in a highly recognized book about Charlemagne that Charlemagne was convinced that the Frankish people were the "God-elect people" of the new age.[20] This idea was expanded to all the Germanic tribes and widely taught in the nineteenth century by highly recognized Lutheran teachers in Germany.[21] It is not difficult to see that some consider this to be an important background for Hitler's ideas of Germanic supremacy and the holocaust.

Constantine, Charlemagne, and a multitude of others give us reason to establish my second statement: *Over a period of centuries, the interpretations of the gospel that prevailed were those linked with the strongest political powers. These powers, which provided leadership and interpretation of Christianity, were not free from wickedness, injustice, and unrighteousness.*

As we investigate the roots of our own history and understand the situation of our day, we cannot ignore one most tragic and fatal fact of history. Obviously, many righteous individuals tried, over the years, to establish a knowledge of Christ's teachings by righteous living and by emulating His example of sacrifice motivated by love. But the fact remains that Christianity has used brutal suppression to destroy opposition and to persecute and even kill those who believed in different interpretations of Christianity. Very few people today recall, for instance, that Theodosius, the Roman emperor who was called "the Great," helped make the Nicene Creed survive by having 30,000 Arian Christians killed during a single night in an amphitheater.[22]

Horst Herrmann, professor of theology at the University of Muenster, wrote in his book *Ketzer in Deutschland:* "If Theodosius would not have been victorious in this battle [the above-mentioned slaughter] and if they would not have continued to fight for their doctrine, then maybe it would have happened that Christianity today would believe in the teachings of Arius" (i.e., Christ being born of a virgin as the literal Son of God, similar in everything with Him but not the same). Then Herrmann continued, "Now every Christian in the world knows, like Bishop Athanasius, that Christ is: . . ." (Herrmann then quoted parts of the Athanasian Creed.) He then concluded, not without sarcasm, "Or maybe he does not know it so precisely. Could it be that the bloody fights for the jota did not pay off after all?"[23]

This sarcasm is understandable when we take into consideration the text of the Athanasian Creed, which still stands for the belief of most of the Christian world. The Athanasian Creed was developed in an attempt to improve the Nicene Creed. The Athanasian Creed reads:

> We worship one God in Trinity, and Trinity in Unity, neither confounding the Persons, nor dividing the Substance. For there is one Person of the Father, another the Son, and another of the Holy Ghost. But the Godhead of the Father, of the Son, and of the Holy Ghost, is all one, the Glory equal, the Majesty co-eternal. Such as the Father is, such is the Son, and such is the Holy Ghost. The Father uncreate, the Son uncreate, and the Holy Ghost uncreate. The Father incomprehensible, the Son incomprehensible, and the Holy Ghost incomprehensible. The Father eternal, the Son eternal, and the Holy Ghost eternal. And yet they are not three eternals, but one eternal. As also there are not three incomprehensibles, nor three uncreated, but one uncreated and one incomprehensible. So likewise the Father is Almighty, the Son Almighty, and the Holy Ghost Almighty. And yet they are not three Almighties, but one Almighty. So the Father is God, the Son is God, and the Holy Ghost is God. And yet they are not three Gods, but one God.

Several hundred years after Theodosius, Charlemagne established Christianity very zealously as a unifying power in his kingdom. When the Saxons did not submit to the emperor's will and become Christians quickly enough, he invited, in A.D. 782, 4,500 noble sons of the Saxons to a meeting in Verden an der Aller. He had all of them killed.[24] This was how Christianity was introduced to my own ancestors.

The Orthodox church of the Middle Ages established the Inquisition for the sole purpose of finding individuals or groups who were not in full obedience and harmony with the established beliefs. The Cathari, the Waldenses, the Begins and the Begards, the Salpeterer, and many others were persecuted and killed, some groups to the very last person. John Huss, the Bohemian theologian who established the motto, "Search the truth, listen to the truth, learn the truth, love the truth, remain true to the truth, defend the truth until death," was burned, and his ashes were scattered in the Rhine River.[25] William Tyndale, who was the first to translate *and* print the New Testament in English, because he believed people should read and study the scriptures themselves, was persecuted because of his translation. Finally church authorities brought him to his death.

The Reformation did not bring a change in attitude. As soon as Reformation churches became established in various places, the reformers and their followers began to identify and search for heretics. Heretics were those who were "different," and so easily called "devilish." As did the medieval church, the reformers and their followers did not hesitate to bring heretics to painful deaths.

Many wars have been fought in the name of religion, with millions losing their lives. I must mention the dreadful night of St. Bartholomew when 13,000 Huguenots were killed in France in one night, including men, women, and children.[26] I mention also the dreadful end that came to Thomas Muenzer and his faithful

ELDER F. ENZIO BUSCHE

peasants. Also, nearly all of the Anabaptists in the city of New Jerusalem (Muenster) were killed and three of their leaders were placed in iron cages and hoisted to the top of the Lamberti church until they died.[27] The cages still hang there. The remnants of this people were led later by a man named Menno Simons and called Mennonites.[28]

A very tragic chapter in the perversion of Christian religion persisted until recent times. Individuals who were not liked or who the authorities decided had caused a problem were called "witches" and were given no mercy. In Germany during the seventeenth century alone, Herrmann estimates no fewer than 300,000 people accused of witchcraft were put to death by burning or beheading.[29]

It seems to be necessary, in light of the confrontations between the peoples of Islam and the West, to recall the eight arrogant, bloody Christian crusades to the Holy Land between A.D. 1095 and 1291. Gerhard Konzelmann, an expert on the Near East and best-selling author, described how the Christian crusaders behaved when they arrived in Jerusalem:

> The knights from Europe changed into the most brutal beasts that ever took lodging in Jerusalem. They surpassed in their cruelty all other conquerors of the past. In the houses and on the streets, they slaughtered the ones with weapons or the ones without, young or old, men or women and children. In the morning of their second day no Moslem and no Jew was still alive in Jerusalem.

Konzelmann finished his report about the "victorious" first crusade with the following statement:

> The horrible massacre of the 15th and 16th of July in 1099 A.D. provided the roots for the opinions of

Moslems about Christians: The Moslems looked at the Europeans from that time on as lustful, murdering bandits without conscience. What happened in those two days burdened the relationship between the people of the Islam faith and the Christian crusaders in a dimension that left no room for reconciliation.[30]

The Mayas, Aztecs, and Incas on the American continent suffered the same fate as the people in Europe suffered at the hands of such leaders as Theodosius and Charlemagne, as the Spanish conquistadors Velazquez, Cortez, and Pizzaro were following their motto, "Brothers—comrades! Let us follow the sign of the Holy Cross in true faith towards victory!"[31]

The famous French explorer and author, Pierre Honore, wrote:

> The reason for the quick destruction of the Indian kingdoms was the deep-rooted, traditional expectation among these ancient people that a white god would return to them. In their humble expectation of the rulership of their god, they became victims and their kingdoms and civilizations were destroyed in blood and smoke.[32]

I can therefore make my third statement safely without being accused of exaggeration: *Christianity has a long history of intolerance toward those holding different opinions. They were persecuted brutally, defamed as devilish, and, in many cases, put to death.*

After all I have said, we can conclude that *we* humans must fail when *we* try to interpret what *we* consider to be gospel truth without relying on a living prophet and divine revelation. The Bible, which for centuries was regarded as the flawless word of God, has become, in the eyes of theologians, archaeologists, and historians, the subject of serious questions about its origin, validity, and authenticity. As the people of our day have become aware of the suppression of early Christian developments and other "fruits" of historical Christianity, they have come to a shocking understanding.

As early as the late seventeenth century, Roger Williams, one of the founding fathers of modern-day Baptists, said, "The church of Christ is not on earth until Christ sends forth new apostles to plant churches anew." The same Roger Williams termed it "blasphemy" to call Europe "Christian."[33]

Even though humans cannot interpret divine truth without divine help, thousands of honest, righteous, and humble people created their own circles of prayer and authored hundreds of different Christian beliefs. With the establishment of the Constitution of the United States, oppressed and frustrated Europeans were given a place of dreams, a place of hope. Concurrent with their immigration to the new continent, the soil was prepared for the Lord himself to restore once again the true order of the priesthood of God and a knowledge of the true interpretation of the plan of salvation.

We should not be surprised to see that the restoration of the true gospel of Jesus Christ, following the humble prayer of a fourteen-year-old youth, has brought suspicion, envy, and fear to some leaders of traditional Christian churches. The early members of the restored Church, which the Lord himself called The Church of Jesus Christ of Latter-day Saints, had to suffer many of the same difficulties as those brave souls who preceded them throughout the history of Christianity. The early members were persecuted, oppressed, and driven from their homes. They were driven from Ohio to Missouri and to Illinois on the Mississippi River. When the first prophet of the Restoration, Joseph Smith, suffered a martyr's death, the disciples of the Lord in the restored Church showed the fruit of their faith. They left their homes again and crossed the plains, the wilderness, and the roadless mountains to settle in the desolation of the barren desert of the West.

To understand the Restoration, we need to be aware of the tragedy of Christian history—not to create ill-feelings or to pass judgment, but to understand that for the first time since shortly after the death of the early disciples of Christ, we have the gospel in its entire purity, undefiled by human ambition and without human interpretation.

Here is an interesting fact. In the same year that the pioneers of the restored Church were spending their first Christmas in their humble quarters in the wilderness of the West in 1847, Karl Marx and Friedrich Engels were writing their Communist Manifesto.[34] We find, in studying the lives of Marx and Engels,[35] that this manifesto resulted in part from analytical observations of the history of the Christian church made by philosophers of the Enlightenment period. Their observations can be exemplified by a statement of the German poet Johann Wolfgang von Goethe that the history of the Christian church is "a mixture of error [Irrtum] and force [Gewalt]."[36]

The millions of members of the restored Church are spread today over all continents, having come from many races and cultures. They are living witnesses of the divine restoration of the power and dignity of the priesthood of God. The Lord has restored the keys to preach the gospel of repentance for the remission of sins. All mankind will have an opportunity to hear this message and will be invited to make a covenant with the living God. Being witnesses gives members of the restored

Church a sacred privilege and obligation to share their new understanding and to show the fruit of the Spirit through their lives.

Yes, we have received a new light. It is, in truth, the old and everlasting light. We have received the keys to the powers of the Holy Spirit. With these powers from above, it is our opportunity and obligation to learn to love every one of our Heavenly Father's children. We are to make the love of Christ the strongest power in this world. As His love emanates through His disciples, reaching eventually to all of our Heavenly Father's children, new hope and new light will penetrate the whole world. The weight of prejudice, ignorance, hate, deception, and fear that seems more than ever to burden relationships between individuals and nations will be overcome.

Men obviously have separated themselves from the clear waters of divine truth. They ignore the message of Christ or give it only lip service. They have made masterful progress in the technical, materialistic world. But without divine light, they succumb all too often to the carnal mind in its drive for expansion, extroversion, and greed. Now the children of God suddenly seem to awaken and seem to panic as they realize that the last possibility of expansion can mean the destruction of mankind, the whole planet on which we live.

In this situation, hope is raised that the message of the restored gospel of Jesus Christ and the radiation of its fruits will eventually help the children of God to find the memory of their true origin and change the direction of their lives. Hope is raised that men will learn to turn their hearts to the only power and strength through which salvation can come—to the Lord, Jesus Christ. Hope is raised that we all will eventually learn through this majestic influence of His spirit radiating from the members of His church—learn to respect one another, to trust, and to love one another. Hope is raised that the ultimate goal of Jesus Christ will finally be established: "Glory to God in the highest, and on earth peace, good will toward men."

NOTES

1. Karl Maly, *Wie enstand das Neue Testament*, 3rd ed. (Stuttgart: Verlag Katholisches Bibelwerk GmbH, 1981), pp. 41–42.
2. Alfons Kemmer, *Das Neue Testament: Eine Einführung für Laien*, 3rd ed. (Freiburg in Breisgau: Verlag Herder, 1980), pp. 16–17.
3. See *Encyclopaedia Britannica*, 1980 ed., 2:939–40, 973.
4. See *Wie enstand das Neue Testament*, p. 47.
5. See *Encyclopaedia Britannica*, 2:941.
6. See Kemmer, *Das Neue Testament*, pp. 22–23.
7. See Karl Kupisch, *Kirchengeschichte* (Stuttgart: Verlag W. Kohlhammer GmbH, 1978), 1:30, 38, 39.
8. See ibid., pp. 30–31.
9. See ibid., p. 33.
10. See ibid., pp. 38–39.
11. See ibid., p. 71.
12. See ibid., pp. 114–16.
13. See Horst Herrmann, *Ketzer in Deutschland*, ed. no. 7185 (Munich, Germany: Verlag Wilhelm Heyne, 1982), pp. 124–25.
14. See ibid., p. 126.
15. See ibid., p. 135.
16. See ibid., pp. 273–75.
17. See ibid., pp. 184–88.
18. See Daryl Chase, *Christianity Through the Centuries* (Salt Lake City: Deseret Book Co., 1944), p. 155.
19. Kupisch, *Kirchengeschichte*, 1:72–73.
20. See Rudolph Wahl, *Karl der Grosse* (Munich: Verlag Bruckmann, 1978), pp. 208, 288, 293.
21. See Ernest Weymar, *Das Selbstverständnis der Deutschen* (Stuttgart: Ernest Klett Verlag, 1961), p. 33.
22. See Herrmann, *Ketzer in Deutschland*, p. 66.
23. Ibid., pp. 66–67.
24. See Kupisch, *Kirchengeschichte*, 1:148.
25. See Herrmann, *Ketzer in Deutschland*, p. 32.
26. See Kupisch, *Kirchengeschichte*, 1975 ed., 4:43.
27. See Herrmann, *Ketzer in Deutschland*, pp. 184–88. See also Kupisch, Kirchengeschichte, 1974 ed., 3:131.

28. See Kupisch, *Kirchengeschichte,* 1974 ed., 3:132. See also Barbara Beuys, *Und wenn die Welt voll Teufel wär* (Hamburg: Verlag Rowohlt, 1982), p. 269.
29. See Herrmann, *Ketzer in Deutschland,* p. 228.
30. Gerhard Konzelmann, *Jerusalem* (Hoffmann und Campe, 1984), pp. 373–74.
31. *Encyclopaedia Britannica,* 5:195.
32. Pierre Honore, *Ich fand den weissen Gott* (Verlag Heinrich Scheffler, 1961), pp. 14–15.
33. Chase, *Christianity Through the Centuries,* pp. 202–3.
34. Günter Brakelmann, *Kirche in Konflikten ihrer Zeit* (Munich: Chr. Kaiser Verlag, 1981), p. 29.
35. See Friedrich Friedenthal, *Karl Marx* (Munich and Zurich: Piper & Co., n.d.).
36. Gerhard Wehr, *Auf den Spuren urchristlicher Ketzer* (Schaffhausen: Novalis Verlag, 1983), p. 21.

OUR MESSAGE TO THE WORLD

ELDER ROBERT E. WELLS

The Church of Jesus Christ of Latter-day Saints has a
unique, three-part, Christ-focused message to the world.

1. THE DIVINE SONSHIP OF JESUS CHRIST

First is the divine Sonship of Jesus Christ, which is
central to understanding the entire plan of salvation. He
is the First Begotten Son of the Father in the premortal
existence and the Only Begotten Son of the Father on
earth. God the Eternal Father is the literal parent of our
Lord and Savior Jesus Christ and of His other spirit children (see 1 Nephi 11:18, 21).[1]

When we refer to the divine Sonship of Jesus Christ,
we are also referring to His role as a God in the premortal
sphere. This Firstborn Son of Elohim the Father was chosen and ordained in the primeval councils in heaven to
be the Savior of the yet-to-be-born race of mortals.[2] Jesus
was also chosen and sent by the Father to organize and
create this earth, our solar system, our galaxy, even
worlds without number.

Jesus Christ was and is Jehovah of the Old Testament, the God of Adam and of Noah, the God of Abraham, Isaac, and Jacob. Jehovah appeared to and talked to the ancient prophets. When He spoke He did so on behalf of the Father, and He said what His Father would have said. Jehovah of the Old Testament became Jesus Christ of the New Testament when He was born into mortality.

The "divine Sonship" also refers to the designation "Only Begotten Son in the flesh." Ancient and modern scriptures use the title "Only Begotten Son" to emphasize the divine nature of Jesus Christ. This title signifies that Jesus' physical body was the offspring of a mortal mother and of an immortal Eternal Father, which verity is crucial to the Atonement, a supreme act that could not have been accomplished by an ordinary man. Christ had power to lay down His life and power to take it up again because He had inherited immortality from His Heavenly Father. From Mary, His mother, Christ inherited mortality, or the power to die.

This infinite atonement of Christ and Christ's divine Sonship go together hand in hand to form the single most important doctrine of all Christianity. Elder Bruce R. McConkie said, "We view the atonement of the Lord Jesus Christ as the center and core and heart of revealed religion."[3] The book of Alma declared, "This is the whole meaning of the law" (34:14).

2. THE DIVINE MISSION OF JOSEPH SMITH AND THE BOOK OF MORMON

The second part of our gospel message and central to the Restoration is the divine mission of Joseph Smith and the Book of Mormon to bring people unto Christ.

We declare that the heavens opened to Joseph Smith and a pillar of light descended brighter than the noonday sun. In that pillar stood two personages—God the Father and His Son, Jesus Christ—whose brightness and glory defied all description. The Father spoke, saying, Joseph, "This is My Beloved Son. Hear Him!" (JS–H 1:17).

One of the hallmarks of the Prophet Joseph Smith's calling was his divine education in the writings and prophecies of the ancient apostles and prophets. The writings and teachings of the Prophet Joseph Smith "read like a seamless gospel fabric, woven from the sacred truths of ancient and modern scripture."[4]

Joseph Smith was much more than an uneducated plowboy of the American frontier. Rather, in the process of his divine education, he received the greatest heavenly tutorials ever given to man. He received direct answer to prayer from God, not from books. After the First Vision he received other visions and numerous visits from angelic ministers, and "he was taught for years by . . . holy angels sent from God out of heaven to teach and instruct him and prepare him to lay the foundation of this Church."[5] The inspiration of the Holy Ghost was likewise fundamental in Joseph's expounding of biblical scripture. He received revelations from Jesus Christ, and the Urim and Thummim provided another means by which Joseph Smith received scriptural instructions.

The eternal truths he taught answered a brood of questions that had been in the minds of philosophers for centuries. When one studies the doctrinal teachings revealed to Joseph Smith, that person, if he or she is sincere in the search for truth, will be led to Jesus Christ and His role as our Savior, Redeemer, and Advocate with the Father. In studying these teachings of Joseph about the Savior, uncertainty and doubt flee, and hearts are changed. The honest person finds greater meaning in life by the Prophet's answers to the philosophical questions, Where did we come from? Why are we here? Where are we going? Because of revelations given to Joseph, the memory veil between this life and our premortal existence becomes almost transparent at times. And the veil between this life and the spirit world becomes thinner, causing family ties to become stronger, sweeter, and more meaningful as the hearts of the children turn to their fathers and the hearts of the fathers turn to their children.

The Prophet Joseph taught that the same sociality that we enjoy in this life will continue into the next, giving great comfort to those seeing friends and loved ones depart from this earth (see D&C 130:2). The doctrines of salvation taught by this prophet distill upon our souls as the very dews from heaven (see D&C 121:45). Joseph taught eternal truths that lead those who hunger and thirst for righteousness to the living Christ and to the bosom of God the Father.

Like Joseph Smith, the Book of Mormon is a divine instrument to draw the reader closer to Christ. It is a collection of writings by prophets who lived in the Western Hemisphere, who believed in Christ, and who prophesied of Christ, some of whom associated with Christ during the brief time He visited the Americas after His resurrection. Those ancient American prophets wrote the Book of Mormon for our day. It has withstood every conceivable test by both skeptical and sincere minds. It is not on trial. We are the ones on trial, being tested by our acceptance or rejection of its truths, teachings, commandments, and declarations (see 2 Nephi 33:11–14).

President Ezra Taft Benson reminded us forcefully that if we forget to teach and preach the Book of

Mormon, and if we forget to study and meditate on the contents of this book of Holy Writ, we will be under condemnation. We have a mission and a commandment to declare its contents to the world and to bear testimony of it (see D&C 84:54–58).

3. THE DIVINE NATURE OF THE CHURCH

Our third declaration is the divine nature of The Church of Jesus Christ of Latter-day Saints to prepare the way for the Second Coming of Christ. This church has received from on high the restoration of the divine authority to have and to exercise the priesthood of Jesus Christ and to use this priesthood in performing the requisite saving ordinances so that they are recorded in heaven as well as on earth.

The restoration referred to was essential to the Second Coming because a study of ecclesiastical history shows that the original laws had been transgressed, the original ordinances had been changed, and the everlasting covenants had been broken, just as Isaiah had prophesied many centuries before (see Isaiah 24:5). Furthermore, Paul had warned that the Second Coming would occur only after a falling away from the original teachings of Christ and the Apostles (see 2 Thessalonians 2:3–4).

To prepare the way for the Second Coming, the Restoration took place—through Joseph Smith—of every necessary doctrine and sacred ordinance given by God to the prophets of past dispensations, including the Christ-focused temple ordinances.

We have, in original form, everything that has ever been brought to earth that is part of the great Plan of Salvation—nothing altered, nothing modified. We believe in the same priesthood authority held by the ancients; the same organization as the primitive Church, headed by apostles and prophets; the same spiritual gifts; the same ancient scriptures as well as new latter-day scriptures—the Book of Mormon, the Doctrine and Covenants, the Pearl of Great Price.

I pray that we each will see how great the importance is to gain an understanding, through diligent and prayerful study, of the divine Sonship of Jesus Christ—the Savior of the world; that Joseph Smith's divine mission was to bring about the restoration of the principles and ordinances of the gospel of Jesus Christ, and also the Book of Mormon, which is indeed another witness that Jesus Christ is the Son of the living God; and that this church—The Church of Jesus Christ of Latter-day Saints—is "the Lord's kingdom once again established on the earth, preparatory to the second coming of the Messiah" (Book of Mormon, Introduction). I so declare in all humility and testimony.

NOTES

1. See James E. Talmage, *The Articles of Faith*, 12th ed. (Salt Lake City: The Church of Jesus Christ of Latter-day Saints, 1924), p. 466.
2. See James E. Talmage, *Jesus the Christ*, 3rd ed. (Salt Lake City: The Church of Jesus Christ of Latter-day Saints, 1916), p. 4.
3. *A New Witness for the Articles of Faith* (Salt Lake City: Deseret Book Co., 1985), p. 81.
4. Richard C. Galbraith, "Joseph Smith and the Holy Scriptures," in *Scriptural Teachings of the Prophet Joseph Smith*, sel. Joseph Fielding Smith (Salt Lake City: Deseret Book Co., 1993), p. 5.
5. Wilford Woodruff, in *Journal of Discourses*, 16:265.

INDEX